Deschutes
Public Library

D0481750

Thank You, Teacher

Thank You, Teacher

GRATEFUL STUDENTS TELL THE STORIES
OF THE TEACHERS WHO CHANGED THEIR LIVES

edited by
Holly & Bruce Holbert

New World Library
Novato, California

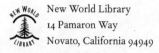 New World Library
14 Pamaron Way
Novato, California 94949

Copyright © 2016 by Holly and Bruce Holbert

All rights reserved. This book may not be reproduced in whole or in part, stored in a retrieval system, or transmitted in any form or by any means — electronic, mechanical, or other — without written permission from the publisher, except by a reviewer, who may quote brief passages in a review.

Page 273 is an extension of this copyright page. Parts of this book were previously published by Kaplan Publishing in a different form in 2010 under the title *Signed, Your Student*.

Text design by Tona Pearce Myers

Library of Congress Cataloging-in-Publication Data is available.

First printing, May 2016
ISBN 978-1-60868-418-2
EISBN 978-1-60868-419-9

Printed in Canada on 100% postconsumer-waste recycled paper

 New World Library is proud to be a Gold Certified Environmentally Responsible Publisher. Publisher certification awarded by Green Press Initiative. www.greenpressinitiative.org

10   9   8   7   6   5   4   3   2   1

This book is dedicated to our parents,
Vince and Margaret Moore,
Bonnie Hogue, and
Pat and Barb Holbert;
and our children,
Natalie, Luke, and Jackson Holbert.

[Contents]

Preface • Bruce Holbert   xiii

Introduction • Holly Holbert   xvii

Dear Teacher • Abraham Lincoln   1

Dear Monsieur Germain • Albert Camus   3

Part One. Grade School

Almost Like Singing • Dr. Maya Angelou,
poet and civil rights activist   7

I Was Your First-Grade Teacher • Andrew Gross, author   9

She Made Me Feel as If the World Was Mine to Conquer •
Gene Simmons, bass guitarist and singer-songwriter   12

She Loved the Boys and Girls of Haldeman • Chris Offutt,
author   14

An Arena for Me to Shine • Melora Hardin, actor   20

I Didn't Know Her First Name • Cecil Murphey, author   22

The Time I Needed • Daisy Martinez,
   chef and TV personality   25

Love of Reading • Sherri Shepherd, actor and comedian   27

Ode to Teachers • Julie Peters, author   29

Mrs. Lane's Olympics • Janet Evans, Olympic athlete   31

Miss Germaine Earth • Gregory Maguire, author   33

Unforgettable • Joan Baker, voice-over actress   36

I Met Her Only Once • Rudy Gaskins, producer   39

What I Remember • Kelli Russell Agodon, poet   42

John Dark • Carol Muske-Dukes, poet and novelist   44

Teachers • C. K. Williams, poet   47

Suzanne Will Be a Writer • Suzanne Harper, author   51

It Only Took Me a Moment or Two to Recognize Him •
   Peter Selgin, author and playwright   55

She Would Invite Me Up to Her Desk • Meg Wolitzer,
   author   60

Part Two. Middle School

He Could Understand • Katherine Marsh, author   65

As Tall as I Would Ever Need to Be • Robert Reich,
   political economist   68

She Had Expectations • Elizabeth McCracken, author   70

All the Lights inside My Head Came On • Anne Perry,
   author   73

An Encouraging Figure • Leslie Epstein, author   75

I Have No Idea What They Saw • Derek Alger, author   79

He Was So Passionate about Reading • CJ Lyons, author   88

Renowned for Her High Standards • Thomas Kane,
   economist   90

He Thought I Was Smart • Alan Dershowitz, lawyer 93

We Knew What Love Was • Alex Shoumatoff, author 95

Part Three. High School

With Love and High Hopes • Mariana Klaveno, actor 99

Full of Thinking and Caring • George Saunders, author 103

I Will Be Forever in Her Debt • Dan Webster, journalist 109

Never without His Hat • Marya Hornbacher, author 112

Shaped and Furiously Polished by My Teachers •
David Bellos, translator and biographer 115

The Writer inside Me • Tess Gerritsen, author 119

He Made Class Fun • Alison Haislip, actor 121

Changing the Face of Rock and Roll • Stewart Lewis,
writer and singer 124

Thank God for English Teachers • John Rosengren,
author 130

I Am Thankful for Her Efforts • Tommy James,
singer-songwriter 132

You Know, I Have No Idea • Stuart Spencer, playwright 133

Keep Going • Gillian Anderson, actor 136

In a Different Way • Faye Kellerman, author 138

Please Use Only Sentences You've Never Heard Before •
John Whalen, poet 140

Forty Years Later • Dan Millman, author 144

Respect • Beau Bridges, actor 147

A "Class Act" • Roy Firestone, sportscaster 149

My Journey with Books • Eric Liebetrau, editor 151

"That" Teacher • Wayne Federman, actor and comedian 155

Not in the Right Neighborhood • Helen Gurley Brown,
  editor in chief 158

Ignited a Fire in Me • John Glenn, astronaut and senator ... 159

Unlimited Opportunities • Sherry Lansing, CEO 161

And So She Read • Bill Moyers, journalist 163

She Was Right • Alethea Black, author 166

Thanks, Mom • Dean Karnazes, ultramarathon runner 169

The Final Piece of the Puzzle • Lee Greenwood, singer 171

A Man of Passion • Darryl Wimberley, author 173

You'll Never Amount to a Hill of Beans • Keith Jackson,
  sportscaster 177

Unquestioned Authority • Robert Pinsky, poet 179

To Be Inspired, to Inspire • Indira Cesarine, photographer ... 181

The Death-Defying Mr. G • William Lashner, author 184

All Things Pass • Anthony Bozza, author 188

He Made Me Feel Valued • Ellie Krieger,
  dietitian and author 192

A World of Possibility • Nicola Kraus, author 194

He Taught Me More Important Life Skills • Brian Crosby,
  author and teacher 197

Don't Know Anyone Like Him • Joe Wilkins, author 200

Ça Va • Rachel Toor, author 204

I Was Mesmerized • Maria Mazziotti Gillan, author 208

He Saved My Life • Hillary Susz, singer and writer 212

Part Four. College

You're Going to Be a Writer • Jess Walter, author 217

A Grandson • Bruce Holbert, teacher and author 222

Made a Lasting Impression • Myles Kennedy, singer   226

He Had Done His Homework about Our Pasts •
    Stephen Dunn, poet   229

Walter Taught Liberation • Rosanne Cash,
    singer-songwriter   232

I Remember the Kindness • Jim Piddock,
    actor and producer   233

My Friend and Teacher • Ken Burns,
    director and producer   237

His Dazzling Language • Peter Coyote, actor and narrator   238

On a Tangent • Jerry Spinelli, author   240

The Man Was Right on the Money • Doug Holder, poet   242

No More Gold Stars • Kris Dinnison, author   244

Home of the Soul • Shann Ray, author   246

Stepping on the Edge of My Doubting • Annie Finch,
    poet and performer   249

A Beloved Teacher Calls My Writing "Fecking Crap" •
    Sharma Shields, author   254

A Mentor and a Friend • Jim Belushi, actor   262

I Had the Good Fortune to Work with Him •
    Gregory Spatz, author   265

Permission Acknowledgments   273

Acknowledgments   275

Index of Contributors   277

About the Editors   279

[Preface]

BRUCE HOLBERT

THIS BOOK WAS BORN in a fashion akin to the birth of my first child. The first labor pains arrived in early morning, and I was the last to know.

On a December night several years ago, Holly woke me, saying she couldn't sleep. I remember checking the clock to see if I had slept through the alarm. It was sometime after 2:00 AM, and sleep was at a premium.

She announced she had decided to write a book for the teachers, "the ones like you no one hears about."

"What?" I asked.

"I was thinking about how you stand out in the hallway between classes to make sure you talk to everybody when they pass by or come into your room. You make jokes with them and their girlfriends or boyfriends. Kids you don't even have in class stop to talk with you. Sometimes you make people feel better, and you don't even know them. I want to see if I can find stories about those teachers."

I'm sure I was not terribly encouraging. I may have yawned and thought: This too shall pass.

When I next woke, though, Holly was already at the computer, and since that morning I'm not sure she has spent a stretch of more than twenty-four hours away from it. She started out with a query letter to prospective contributors filled with such regard for me and written in such sincere language that even if the project had not progressed any further, the letter itself would have been a gift as generous as any I've been given. It seemed to me, though, that the letter's moving qualities spelled out the project's doom. No one would respond to a query that didn't include who would possess the international rights and where each contributor's name might appear on the jacket.

I was wrong.

Stories began arriving a week later. Janet Reno called, and I didn't take the call because the caller ID read simply RENO and I thought she was selling time-shares. The kids raced to the mailbox because no one knew when John Glenn or Beau Bridges or Jim Belushi might drop us a line. Those who could not contribute often wrote or called to encourage Holly and to send me their best wishes. This was the most compelling, unintended consequence of the project. People wanted to honor their teachers, yes, but they were just as anxious to respond to Holly's genuine desire to do something significant for me. What she felt for the work I have cared about and committed to for more than thirty years — work she saw as too often unappreciated — so moved those she solicited that they volunteered their time and words in response to her resolve and faith in education in general and me in particular. I am honored.

It should not have surprised me. Almost every story in this book is told in the context of successful people recalling teachers who were willing to purchase, with time and effort, stock in their lives before they themselves knew they were worthy of the marketplace. As a result, these students purchased larger stakes in their own lives and made good on their teachers' investments. That is the genius of the best teachers. One may teach the most demanding class in the school; another may have little concern for grades at all. But if they are like the teachers portrayed in this book, their students understand: these teachers' demands are efforts to demonstrate to their students the talents and character they are not yet aware they possess.

As with my children's births, my wife bore the labor of this book, and I coaxed a little at the end. However, that does not preclude me from having hopes for both.

For teachers, I hope they will recognize themselves in these stories. I can see almost everyone I work with in one or another.

For students and parents, I hope the same, that they will also see their teachers in these pages, because they are there. In my career, I have had the good fortune to teach great kids. Many are generous enough to write or stop at my classroom and express their thanks as they progress. For those kids, perhaps, I was a voice that spoke to them for the weeks or months when hearing someone's voice could move them forward in their lives. Though it would gratify my ego to be the person to whom each responded in such a manner, I know I am not. I take much solace in that knowledge, however, as I consistently witness students in other classes finding themselves through other teachers' efforts, some polar opposites of myself in our notions of how to run a classroom. I have encountered no one in this profession who has failed to affect at least a student or two in significant ways; most teachers do so every day, just as the teachers described in this book have.

I hope, finally, that if those who have little or no connection to schools stumble upon these stories, these pages will provide enough light to balance the dark aspersions that the media and politics often cast on my profession. I hope too that these readers will be reminded of the paradox education researchers consistently report: while respondents typically report that educators in this country perform unsatisfactorily, they just as characteristically rate their children's teachers as above average or excellent. The public approves of the teachers who instruct our children every day yet disparage the more general notion of educators that the media and political wonks tell us are the reason for society's ills. This is the uncomfortable irony in which teachers exist.

[Introduction]

HOLLY HOLBERT

MY HUSBAND, BRUCE, has been a high school English and social studies teacher for more than thirty years. In that time he has received countless letters from students and parents thanking him for the effect he has had on their lives. Yet even with all this gratitude, he still hesitates when someone asks what he does for a living.

Every day in the newspaper, Bruce reads about low test scores, about teachers who are incompetent or who take advantage of their students. Letters to the editor typically assail everyone in the profession for assigning too much homework or not enough, for doling out too much discipline or not enough. What we don't hear much about are those teachers like Bruce who quietly go about affecting thousands of children's lives for the good. Instead of holding teachers in the highest regard and vigorously recruiting the best people for the job, as some countries do, we pay teachers lower wages than the average college graduate and think of them as hired hands.

Bruce's first teaching job was in Jerome, Idaho, a small town of around seven thousand. His base salary was $8,500 a year, barely enough for rent, food, and utilities. The school was so overcrowded that he had forty students in his classroom and only thirty desks. The first year of teaching is legendary for its difficulty. Bruce always says that in his first year he learned everything he knew he never wanted to do again. He coached three sports and came home exhausted. The next year, he moved to St. John, Washington, to be closer to family. We were married soon after, and I can't remember how many times during that first year I came home to find him so exhausted he could hardly get off the couch. He wasn't sure if he was being too hard or too easy on his students. He didn't know if he was teaching them the things they needed to learn or if they were even getting it. He still worries about those things. I suppose all good teachers do.

I was at the school one day early in his first year when one of Bruce's students approached him. She couldn't read some of the comments on her paper and didn't know why she had gotten a C. He said, "Well, maybe you're right. Can I read it again and then talk to you about it tomorrow?"

One of the many things that has made Bruce stand out among his peers is his lack of ego in such matters. He will always barter over a higher grade with a student if it means that the student will feel motivated to meet his standards and will feel part of what he calls his "community." Whether in teaching or in any other area of his life, Bruce is always willing to listen and think about the other side of an issue.

In St. John we lived in a small trailer within walking distance of the school. I remember the two of us sitting in the living room the night before homecoming and hearing voices outside. The next moment there were forty kids making a serpentine through our front door and out the back. Kids called or came over to our house two or three nights a week for one thing or another. Bruce understood them, and they recognized that. This is not to say that Bruce was the only person in the school with such traits. He always says that he is most motivated to hold up his end, just as his peers and those who preceded him have done.

Bruce has always practiced the craft of writing as well as teaching it. In 1987 he applied to the University of Iowa Writers' Workshop, where he got to live his art and to talk about writing with people who were doing the same. There we met friends who have become family to us; all of them encouraged Bruce to go east to New York or at least to stay at the university, where he would likely find a teaching job. But Bruce decided to return to St. John, mostly because he had promised his freshman class he would be back and also because he found that the isolation of a university, for him, lacked the quality of spirituality that he got from teaching.

Each year the senior class in St. John chooses a person they admire to speak at their graduation. Bruce was asked by several different classes to speak, including one year when he was still in Iowa, when for the first time in St. John high school history, the graduation speech was in the form of a letter written by a teacher and read by the class president.

Fast-forward many years. Bruce has published almost a dozen short stories and two novels and cowritten two books with me. He teaches now in a much larger school in Spokane, fifty miles north of St. John. We have our own three great kids: Natalie is twenty-four, Luke twenty-three, and Jackson twenty-one. But Bruce's students, current and former, still call, Facebook, and email regularly. He has paid rent on an apartment for a girl left homeless for four months, helped those wanted by the police to turn themselves in with dignity, taken in many of "his kids," some for a few days, some for months at a time. He's brought food for his pregnant students and visited his boys in jails and hospitals. He's written hundreds of letters of recommendation for colleges, jobs, and, sadly, to judges whom he must try to convince to coordinate jail sentences with finishing school.

A few years ago a seventeen-year-old boy in the high school where Bruce taught killed his own parents and then came to school as if nothing had happened. The boy's mother was a math teacher at a high school where Bruce had worked two years earlier. The police found the parents' bloody bodies inside a tractor's bucket.

A few hours later, outside Bruce's classroom, three squad cars surrounded a mideighties compact in the student parking lot. The number of police officers struck him as unusual. The kids speculated drugs or a stolen ATM machine. None of us yet knew that the police had arrested a boy in the classroom next to Bruce's own for double homicide.

The student's friends were quietly plucked from different rooms in the building and informed of the situation by counselors. They were given time to call parents and offered support either through the school's resources or professional people within the community. No one else knew the details except those closest to the boy. His girlfriend had been informed, and the boy had been escorted downtown to be booked.

The next few days at school were difficult, as you might guess. Teachers hovered, checking on kids who were having a hard time and collecting funds for the only other child in the family, a twenty-year-old girl, who not only had to cope with the loss of both parents but also had to come to grips with the fact that her brother was the culprit.

Students, teachers, administrators, and counselors, as well as the police and emergency responders, performed far beyond their job descriptions in those days. They placed the needs of their students ahead of their own lives and turned a horror story into a tragedy with some chance for redemption, if not for the culprit then at least for the student body as a whole. No one told any of the staff to act in this way because they didn't need to be told. It's how the bulk of them behave every day. Yet, you learn nothing from the papers or television of these kinds of efforts to hold together the community.

When I proposed the book you're holding in your hands, Bruce was flattered, I think, but had little hope the project would sprout wings and fly. He suggested I contact some notable people around the Spokane area; maybe one or two of them might give me a story. I began by emailing a few local authors. A local YA author called me within a half hour of receiving my email. He said he thought it was a great idea and asked how I was going to promote it. I told him my ideas; he thought I was thinking too small. He suggested that I contact people across the country and see what the response was. I could always narrow my scope later if I had a hard time getting stories nationally.

Bruce and the kids and I brainstormed and made a list of people we would like to ask to contribute, and I began sending emails and a few letters via the post office the following February. Within a week, Maya Angelou's assistant called. Within three weeks I had stories from Jim Belushi, Jerry Spinelli, and Beau Bridges. The response has continued to be amazing. I have received more than 150 stories from people in all walks of life. It has been so fun to open up my email and letters every day, not knowing what I will find. One day in the spring of 2009, I grabbed the mail before picking up my three children from school. Shuffling through the letters while waiting for them in front of the school, I found a letter and story from former astronaut and senator John Glenn. When my kids got in the car I showed them the letter — it was like Christmas morning for them.

As the stories filtered in, the book's themes began to take shape. The stories were personal and heartfelt. Some people wrote about teachers who had helped guide them through their early childhood years. Others wrote about their personal struggles and the teacher who had helped them through. A few wrote about the tough teachers who made a difference, but most wrote about a teacher who changed the course of their lives and was a big reason they became the accomplished adults they are today.

DEAR TEACHER,

Please teach my son.
He will have to learn, I know,
that all men are not just, all men are not true.
But teach him also that for every scoundrel there is a hero;
that for every selfish politician, there is a dedicated leader...
Teach him for every enemy there is a friend,
Steer him away from envy, if you can,
teach him the secret of quiet laughter.

Let him learn early that the bullies are the easiest to lick...
Teach him, if you can, the wonder of books...
But also give him quiet time
to ponder the eternal mystery of birds in the sky,
bees in the sun, and the flowers on a green hillside.

In the school teach him it is far more honourable to fail than
   to cheat...

Teach him to have faith in his own ideas,
even if everyone tells him they are wrong…
Teach him to be gentle with gentle people,
and tough with the tough.

Try to give my son the strength not to follow the crowd
when everyone is getting on the band wagon…
Teach him to listen to all men…
but teach him also to filter all he hears on a screen of truth,
and take only the good that comes through.

Teach him if you can, how to laugh when he is sad…
Teach him there is no shame in tears,
Teach him to scoff at cynics and to beware of too much
        sweetness…
Teach him to sell his brawn and brain to the highest bidders
but never to put a price-tag on his heart and soul.

Teach him to close his ears to a howling mob
and to stand and fight if he thinks he's right.
Treat him gently, but do not cuddle him,
because only the test of fire makes fine steel.

Let him have the courage to be impatient,
let him have the patience to be brave.
Teach him always to have sublime faith in himself,
because then he will have sublime faith in mankind.

This is a big order, but see what you can do…
He is such a fine fellow, my son!

                              Sincerely, Abraham Lincoln

[Dear Monsieur Germain]

ALBERT CAMUS

19 NOVEMBER 1957

Dear Monsieur Germain,

I let the commotion around me these days subside a bit before speaking to you from the bottom of my heart. I have just been given far too great an honour, one I neither sought nor solicited.

But when I heard the news, my first thought, after my mother, was of you. Without you, without the affectionate hand you extended to the small poor child that I was, without your teaching and example, none of all this would have happened.

I don't make too much of this sort of honour. But at least it gives me the opportunity to tell you what you have been and still are for me, and to assure you that your efforts, your work, and the generous heart you put into it still live in one of your little schoolboys who, despite the years, has never stopped being your grateful pupil. I embrace you with all my heart.

Albert Camus

[PART ONE]

Grade School

DR. MAYA ANGELOU

poet and civil rights activist

ANNIE HENDERSON AND MISS FLOWERS

Stamps, Arkansas

AT THE AGE OF THREE, my brother Bailey (who nicknamed me Maya) and I were sent to live with our grandmother Annie Henderson and my uncle Willie in Stamps, Arkansas, a town of about five thousand. The four of us lived in the rear of the general store, which was owned and operated by my grandmother. My grandmother was really my most important teacher. Although she was not formally educated herself, she taught my brother and me the times tables and how to read, using old school primers and, most important, the Bible.

Like those of most good teachers, her most important lessons didn't come from a book. She taught me how to be a human being, to have dignity, and that it was never appropriate to whine or complain. Customers would come into the store on the hottest day of the year, and my grandmother would take care of them while they complained about the weather. After they left she would whisper, "Did you hear her, all that whining. There are people all over the world who don't have food to eat or blankets to keep them warm. See what you have, and never whine or complain; protest, yes, but never whine."

When I was seven, my brother and I moved to St. Louis to live with my mother and her boyfriend. When my brother and I returned to live with my grandmother, I was so traumatized by that span, I was mute.

It was then that my grandmother introduced me to another woman who became my teacher. Bertha Flowers was a wealthy, educated black woman. She was our side's answer to the richest white woman in town. Miss Flowers divided her time between her main home in Pine Bluff, Arkansas, and her summer home in Stamps. She had two sons; one was a leading civil rights lawyer, and the other was a doctor.

Miss Flowers would come to purchase items from the store and ask that I deliver them. Before those visits my grandmother would remind me, out of respect, to change into my good clothes, not my Sunday best, but good clothes. At her house, Miss Flowers would serve me cookies and lemonade and read aloud from great works, including *A Tale of Two Cities*. Although I had read the book, this was the first instance I had heard the words aloud. Miss Flowers was nearly singing. I wanted to look at the pages. Were they the same I had read? She gave me a book of poems and asked me to memorize one and read it to her on her next visit, and this is how I began to speak once more.

DR. MAYA ANGELOU (1928–2014) was a prominent and beloved African American writer. She was an author, poet, playwright, dancer, speaker, and producer and played an important role in the civil rights movement. Her work, including the autobiography *I Know Why the Caged Bird Sings*, is taught in high schools all over America.

ANDREW GROSS
author

ROSEMARY GUMPEL
first grade, Barnard School for Boys, New York, New York

MY FONDEST MEMORY of a teacher's most meaningful effect on me doesn't go back very far.

As a boy I went to a small private school outside New York City. At that time (the early sixties) it was all about tiny classes, woeful athletics, and crew-cut predominantly Jewish kids whose most flagrant acts of defiance included removing their ties on school grounds.

What I most remember about first grade is learning the rudiments of arithmetic and penmanship from a kindly Englishwoman named Rosemary Gumpel, who taught us manners and civility and treated us goofy, giggling miscreants in an unnaturally adult way. The truth is, not a single well-defined scene from that time filters through — other than hiding rock-hard mashed potatoes from the cafeteria in my blazer pocket one day and facing the consequences by being held back from recess. My penmanship has eroded into an illegible scratch, but I do manage to shift unwanted food to the side of my plate.

Amid the memory haze, somehow I know that that June I was jettisoned off to the second grade feeling a bit more individualistic and mature.

Fast-forward fifty years. I was giving a luncheon talk at a local French restaurant; there were maybe thirty people in the room. After I finished, an elegant, slightly familiar-looking white-haired woman stepped up to me. "Do you remember me, Andy Gross?" she asked.

I looked into her kindly eyes and apologetically shook my head.

She smiled and told me, "I was your first-grade teacher."

Something inside me started to fall apart, like columns of some ancient temple or palace collapsing at the whim of the gods. I don't know what it was — seeing the long passage of time on Miss Gumpel's face or realizing she probably saw the same on mine. She told me how the years had passed for her, recalling that my class was her first teaching assignment, then ticked off incredibly vivid memories of me as a bratty six-year-old: how I was "cute" and "feisty" (*me?*) with impeccable penmanship and how I loved to eat, "though I was so thin." (I decided not to remind her about the mashed potatoes!) I was always "challenging," she said, "and, dare I say it, one of my favorites…"

I was stunned that she could pick me out after fifty years. That she could pick up a book cover in a store and look at the author photo and recall his traits as a child. I realized that this is what a teacher has as their equity — not just names and flickering faces and grades, passed along from year to year but children, people, recognized and remembered after a lifetime, kids who would leave behind their giggly selves and amount to something. They would marry and have families, careers, and children of their own, and I saw how this long, linear journey started somewhere. She boasted a bit, unaware of the twenty years I spent pursuing other dreams: "I always knew you'd become a writer."

I looked at her, and in that instant I realized how much a part of this woman I had become. I held back my tears.

So now my first-grade teacher and I keep in touch. Occasionally I hear updates from some of her other students, classmates of mine I lost touch with a lifetime ago. And my own memories have come back, of who I was — a gangly stick who became a man, who had a career, raised a family, learned to write books — seen through a prism of a teacher I had long forgotten, who saw promise in a young boy, fifty years earlier.

Thank you, Rosemary Gumpel.

ANDREW GROSS is the author of five *New York Times* bestsellers, most recently *One Mile Under*. He lives in Westchester County, New York, with his wife, Lynn. They have three children.

She Made Me Feel as If the World Was Mine to Conquer

GENE SIMMONS

bass guitarist and singer-songwriter, Queens, New York

WHEN I WAS A CHILD OF NINE, I met the first great person in my life. I would forever use her as the needle of my moral compass, of my never-ending passion to learn, and of my work ethic. That person was my teacher.

Her name will be kept confidential. But her memory will be with me for the rest of my life.

At nine years old, I had a really thick Hungarian accent. I felt like an outsider, and I felt unwelcome in a new country I knew nothing about. After the school day ended, she would often take great pains to speak to me about my self-esteem, about how special I was, about all sorts of things the school simply did not teach. There wasn't a class called Self-Esteem. If there had been, my teacher would have taught the master class.

Because of her I used to walk home from grade school feeling as if the world was mine to conquer. Ultimately, it was — and I did, in my own way. The truth is, I wouldn't have been able to without my beloved sixth-grade teacher. Eventually, and ironically, I would teach the sixth grade myself — in Spanish Harlem, in New York City. If I were able to instill that precious self-esteem in just one of my students, I would like to feel that my own sixth-grade teacher would be proud of that.

She will be forever etched in my heart and soul.

GENE SIMMONS is an Israeli American rock bass guitarist, singer-songwriter, record producer, entrepreneur, actor, and television personality. Known by his stage persona the Demon, he is the bass guitarist and co–lead singer of Kiss, the rock band he cofounded in the early 1970s. With Kiss, Simmons has sold more than 100 million albums worldwide.

MRS. JAYNE LIVED ALL HER LIFE in Morehead, and if she had not always been content, she'd made her peace long ago. Occasionally she'd tell a story about going to Lexington with her girlfriends, referring to the trip as "a bunch of country women on the loose." Mrs. Jayne was my first-grade teacher.

She loved the boys and girls of Haldeman, and we loved her back in the fierce way of children who express elemental emotion with every cell in their bodies. Her house held photographs of people she'd taught, their spouses, their babies, their grandchildren. She was a widow with no kids of her own, and her former students served as family. Each year I sent Mrs. Jayne a Christmas card. I visited when I went home and I'd introduced her to Rita. All my grandparents were dead. I only met two of them, and rarely saw them. I wanted Sam and James to know Mrs. Jayne.

I drove to her house, thinking of the car I owned in college, a red Maverick that leaked Bondo at the seams. To save money, I parked in Mrs. Jayne's driveway, which was a block from campus. She said she liked seeing the car and knowing one of her first graders had made it to college.

Now Mrs. Jayne was in her eighties. She never locked her door and was hard of hearing. To visit, you walked into her breezeway and began calling yoo-hoo to avoid startling her. Today she didn't answer and I found her asleep in an easy chair. I gazed around the living room at all the photographs, including one of my sons propped on the mantel. When I was a kid her house was the most proper I'd ever been inside, containing stiff furniture that was uncomfortable to sit on. Later I understood that she lived among lovely antiques that she kept neat and clean, despite using them daily. Now I recognized that everything was a little messy — a pillow on the floor, a rumpled afghan, a water stain on an end table. I tiptoed out. The kids were disappointed and I told them we'd visit the Rowan County Public Library.

I was the first kid who entered the library when it opened in 1967. The head librarian was Frankie Calvert, related by marriage to Mrs. Jayne. One woman taught me to read and the other placed books in my hands each week. I loved them as a child and my devotion has never faltered.

Due to the library's limited holdings, you could only check out four books per library card. Since I read one book per day, and two during school vacation and weekends, I circumvented the rules by getting library cards for all my siblings, two of whom were not yet in school, as well as a card in the name of the family dog. My mother went to town every Saturday for groceries. She dropped me at the library, where I borrowed twenty books, piled them in a heavy grocery bag, and waited for her to retrieve me. By age ten I knew the Dewey Decimal System inside and out.

Now I entered the library with great enthusiasm. A woman from Haldeman was working there and I asked about her family. She hadn't changed much and I wondered if she thought the same of me. Frankie came out of her office and we hugged briefly. A part of me expected her to be thirty years younger. Frankie possessed a lilting accent native to the hills. It is impossible to duplicate in writing, but Frankie looked at my sons and said, "They sure are good-looking boys." She pronounced "boys" with two syllables, as if it were spelled "bo-eeze." Another mountain trait is repetition and she said it again, carrying me into the past and hearing her tell my mother the same about me.

Frankie showed Sam to the children's section, where he began browsing with the experience of a seasoned library kid. James shyly took her hand as she led him to a special spot. She perched on the edge of a tiny chair, leaned forward with a book in her hands, and read aloud to James. He stared at her face, enraptured by her attention. I recalled listening to her in the same way at his age. When Frankie read to me, she'd been younger than I was now. I felt as if time had altered from a linear progression to one of overlapping concentric rings. I felt as if I'd never left Morehead, but been bumped ahead, with remnants of memory all around me.

I wandered the library, stunned to realize that no one else was there on a Saturday afternoon. During college I had put on magic shows for children here, using tricks I'd made from how-to books. The illusions were simple — cut and restored rope, the production of scarves from an empty tube, a magic bag that contained eggs. The magic books were gone, hopefully to a child busy at home folding cardboard into secret gimmicks. I discovered a cache of battered books I dimly recognized. I opened one and discovered a check-out card in the pocket. The signature was mine, dated 1968.

Holding a book that had passed through my hands so long ago gave me a sudden chill that drifted into bliss. The protagonist's name was Eddie. He liked to write notes and post them in his house. I did the same, taping my words to various places in our home. I remembered his dog's name, his best friend's name, his enemy's name. In books I found friends, people who understood me, kids who shared my interest, adults who appreciated me.

I pulled the oldest books from the shelf and examined each card. Several bore my name from thirty years before, and I made a pile of these books for Sam, enthralled that he would read them at the same age. I realized that my signature indicated no new card had ever been required. Don't be sad, I told myself. That's why you came home — to help fix problems like this.

We checked out the books and walked into the heat of summer. The hills were dulled by the humidity that hung in the air like old breath. Sam was disappointed in the library. He had carefully looked over the books and found nothing contemporary, nothing similar to what he'd been reading for the past year. I gave him the Eddie books.

We returned to visit Mrs. Jayne who yoo-hooed back, fully awake now. I hugged her and she felt fragile as papyrus. She'd lost weight and her clothes didn't fit, reminding me that she'd always taken great care of her appearance. She insisted on sitting in the backyard to receive summer guests. The boys adored her as if they'd known her all their lives. She sent me inside to pour glasses of "co-cola" for everyone. The kitchen smelled terrible. Dirty dishes filled the sink. The garbage had not been emptied in a long time. Mrs. Jayne was no longer my first-grade teacher, but an old lady who lived alone and wasn't able to take care of herself.

I scrubbed some glasses, poured drinks for everyone, and carried them outside. Mrs. Jayne was talking to the boys with such care that I suddenly understood why children were drawn to her. She would never judge a child, never criticize, never tamper with innocence. She behaved as if every child was her particular favorite. She still treated me that way and I still basked in her attention.

I motioned Rita inside and showed her the state of the house. She said, "I'll clean the bathroom, you do the kitchen." We found supplies and worked for a couple of hours. I was tidying the living room when Sam and James entered the house with fearful expressions. I asked what was the matter and Sam spoke, taking the lead as oldest, the way I always had as a child.

"Something's wrong with Mrs. Jayne."

"She might be dead," James said.

Tears flowed over his cheeks as he rushed to me and hugged my waist. I called for Rita, who sat with James on the couch while I went to the backyard. Mrs. Jayne sat in her chair asleep. I took the empty glasses inside and made the boys laugh with the truth of Mrs. Jayne. We walked to the car, but I didn't like leaving her in the yard in case the weather shifted or the sunlight burned her pale skin. I went back through the breezeway to help her in the house. Her eyes fluttered open.

"Well, Chris," she said. "What a wonderful surprise. Sit down and let's have a visit."

"Okay."

"When are you bringing those boys of yours for me to meet?"

"Let's go inside, Mrs. Jayne."

"We'll have us some co-cola."

"I can't stay too long."

"You have a busy life now, Chris. There's one thing I

want you to know. I'm just so proud of you for teaching at Morehead. I want you to park in my driveway. It'll be easy for you to walk to work. I like seeing a man's car in the driveway."

"Okay, Mrs. Jayne."

We walked inside, where she eased into her chair, reminding me of a feather pillow slowly settling into utter comfort. Within a few minutes she was asleep again. On my way out I stopped in the breezeway. Leaning against the wall were alphabet posters that had hung in my first-grade classroom, and I remembered writing words that began with each letter. I drove home, understanding that naively and perhaps foolishly, I wanted life in Rowan County to be the same as thirty years ago. I wanted Frankie to give me books and Mrs. Jayne to be healthy.

Later Sam said he didn't like the Eddie books because they were too much like the old days. He wanted to read about the world of today.

CHRIS OFFUTT grew up in Haldeman, Kentucky, a former mining town of two hundred people in the Daniel Boone National Forest. He is the author of two memoirs, *The Same River Twice* and *No Heroes*; two collections of short stories, *Kentucky Straight* and *Out of the Woods*; and one novel, *The Good Brother*. His newest book is *My Father, the Pornographer* (2016). Offutt's work has appeared in *Best American Short Stories* and *Best American Essays*, and he has written screenplays for HBO's *True Blood* and *Treme* and for Showtime's *Weeds*. He lives near Oxford, Mississippi.

[An Arena for Me to Shine]

MELORA HARDIN
actor

MRS. STORY
third grade, Toluca Lake Elementary, North Hollywood, California

MY THIRD-GRADE TEACHER was Mrs. Story, at Toluca Lake Elementary, a sweet public school in the San Fernando Valley in Los Angeles. At the end of every year Mrs. Story had her students recite their favorite poem in front of the class. Being a professional actor from the time I was six years old, I was very excited about this and prepared long and hard. I wanted to win the prize, a book of my choice. I really wanted a book about drawing animals. My favorite poem was "The Raggedy Man": "The Raggedy Man, / He worked with Pa, / He was the goodest man you ever did saw." I wore my overalls, and my mom had styled my hair into two braids. I recited the whole poem with a southern accent, and a southern character to go along with it. It was so exciting to be up in front of my fellow classmates doing something I knew I was good at. It was fun and playful, and it made me connect to that poem in a special way. I remember everything about that day, and I still remember that poem. I won and I got my book, *How to Draw Animals*, which

I still have somewhere. Mrs. Story created an arena for me to shine. I don't think I was the only kid who enjoyed it. It was ingenious to have children memorizing poetry at eight, and it gave me my first taste of what would grow into a real passion for poetry.

Mrs. Story seemed quiet to my eight-year-old self. She seemed old and old-fashioned. I wonder now how old she really was. But she had a twinkle in her eye when it came to English, writing, and literature. We could all feel her passion, and it was transferred to us kids. I was not an early reader and I believe it was in Mrs. Story's class that I really began to enjoy reading for the story and the essence of the piece and finally got beyond the words and the exercise of reading. Mrs. Story's creative way of helping us to connect with the words and their meaning will stay with me forever. I see that day in my mind's eye as a shining example of how a teacher can imprint the mind of a child with joy, curiosity, and excitement. This curiosity and hunger for details and textures have bled over into all that I read. Teachers have the opportunity to shape and sculpt each generation to be more curious, more imaginative, and more specific, and to ask more questions. These are qualities not only of a healthy adult mind but also of a healthy culture and a healthy society. Teachers are heroes!

MELORA HARDIN is a professional dancer, singer, and actor. She appeared in *The Office* as former corporate manager Jan Levinson and is currently appearing as Tammy in the Amazon original series *Transparent*.

I NEVER KNEW MRS. LEAMER'S FIRST NAME, but I remember her well. She became our substitute teacher my first day in third grade. She had light freckles and sandy-colored hair, and she wore thick glasses. When she spoke to me, even at age nine I felt she focused her full attention on me.

I can't remember anything Mrs. Leamer taught me; however, I can never forget the lessons I learned. I was a shy, skinny boy whose clothes never fit properly. What few "new" clothes I had, Mom bought at a secondhand store, or they were hand-me-downs from neighbors. Mrs. Leamer didn't seem to pay attention to my clothes, though.

One Friday she asked me to stay after school. As soon as the other students had left, she handed me a book. "I took this from the big library for you." Both of us knew that no students checked out books from the big library until fourth grade.

"It's written at a fifth-grade level," she said, "but I think you can read it. At least, I'd like you to try."

I stared at the book and read the title: *Father's Big Improvements.*

I thanked her (at least I hope I did) and raced from the room. I didn't even wait until I got home to start the book. As I walked the eleven blocks to our house, I read the first two chapters. I had trouble with a few words, but she was right: I could read the book. On Monday morning, I handed it back to her. "It was good. It was about the father who lived on an old farm and put in electricity and learned to operate a gasoline-powered plow."

She patted my arm. "I knew you could read it."

The following Friday after the final bell rang and all my classmates had rushed into the hallway, Mrs. Leamer handed me another book. This time she only smiled and walked away. It was Booth Tarkington's *Penrod.*

I don't know for how many weeks this went on, but just before Christmas vacation she handed me another book, a children's version of Grimm's *Fairy Tales.* "You might want to read this during your vacation."

I smiled gratefully and clasped the book in my hands.

When school started in January, we had a different teacher. I laid the book on her desk when she wasn't looking. I never saw Mrs. Leamer again. I'm sure I missed her, but life moved on quickly in third grade.

Long after I became an adult, I still thought of Mrs. Leamer. I couldn't remember anything we studied, but I vividly remembered what she did for me. The books, although important, weren't the most important thing she did for me. She made school a haven for me, or as I sometimes think of it today, a safe place.

Without her ever saying these words, Mrs. Leamer made me feel accepted and valued. She didn't see only a shy, skinny kid but instead focused on my potential — not just who I was but who I could be. Home was a place of beatings and drunkenness, a place of yelling and unhappiness. My father drank often and sometimes became violent. That fall a serious illness kept him out of work for months. Yet when I walked into Mrs. Leamer's classroom, I could push that part of my life to the side. For those hours, I escaped loneliness, poverty, and isolation. I was safe, and someone cared about me. Beginning with those days in third grade and continuing all the way through high school, once I walked inside the school building I tuned out my miserable home life.

Years later, I tried to locate that special teacher; however, the school system no longer kept records dating back that far. Even though she was in my life for a mere three months, she had given me hope.

That's how life operates, isn't it? Through the years, God has sent people into my life — individuals like Mrs. Leamer — to nurture and encourage me. Those special individuals enabled me to inch toward feeling accepted and worthwhile.

I never knew Mrs. Leamer's first name, but I know God does. I felt as if God used several special people to prepare me for wholeness and acceptance. One of those individuals who helped was a woman whose first name I never learned.

CECIL (CEC) MURPHEY has written or cowritten more than 135 books, including the *New York Times* bestseller *90 Minutes in Heaven* (with Don Piper) and *Gifted Hands: The Ben Carson Story* (with Dr. Ben Carson). His books have sold in the millions and have brought hope and encouragement to countless people around the world. Visit www.cecilmurphey.com for more information.

[The Time I Needed]

DAISY MARTINEZ
chef and TV personality

MRS. SHARLON
first grade, PS 42, Staten Island, New York

FROM GRADE SCHOOL through high school, college, and even culinary school, I have always been blessed with teachers who are passionate about what they do. It is probably the reason I remember them today; they got such joy from what they did.

Since I never attended kindergarten, and didn't speak English, first grade was a trying experience. I was the only non-English-speaking person, and my poor teacher, Mrs. Sharlon, certainly had her work cut out for her. I remember her standing by my desk, showing me how to fold my paper into four columns and teaching me what it meant to "vote."

We had a piano in the classroom, and Mrs. Sharlon taught us songs (which I learned phonetically at first), and then we would skip to the music, in single-file around the classroom.

She took the extra time that I needed, teaching me to read, to enunciate, to learn English; most important, she taught me a love of reading, which I value to this day. There was never a "stupid" question. It was okay to "color outside the lines," and by the end of first grade, I had the highest reading level in the class. I still remember the hug of pride she gave me when my dad and I went in for our parent-teacher conference.

I left PS 42 in Staten Island, New York, after the fourth grade, and at that time I wasn't mature enough to let Mrs. Sharlon know the great impact that her love of teaching had on me, but to this day I remember her kindness, her patience, and the enthusiasm that she mustered each and every day, in front of twenty-four six-year-olds, one of whom couldn't speak a word of English.

DAISY MARTINEZ is an actor, model, chef, television personality, and author. She hosts the PBS television series *Daisy Cooks!* Her show *Viva Daisy!* launched on the Food Network in 2009.

SHERRI SHEPHERD
actor and comedian

MRS. LOSHESKA
fourth grade, Chicago, Illinois

I STILL REMEMBER MY FOURTH-GRADE TEACHER, Mrs. Losheska (I'm sure I've butchered her name!). I lived in the inner city, so all the little girls looked forward to being in Mrs. Losheska's class because she was the pretty blond white woman who'd let us comb through her silky hair. I'm sure that's why I wear long-haired wigs to this day!

At 4:00 PM every day, Mrs. Losheska would have us all relax at our desks while she read to us. She was a master at voices and would take us to unexplored worlds. I remember looking at the clock in anticipation, waiting to hear all the different characters in Mrs. Losheska's books. My love of reading was instilled by Mrs. Losheska.

To this day, I love to escape in the afternoons with a good book. I love to read to my son. I too use different voices, the way Mrs. Losheska did, and I hope that I too can instill that same joy of reading in my son.

SHERRI SHEPHERD is a stand-up comedian and actor and a former co-host on the ABC daytime talk show *The View*. She also appeared on Broadway in Rodgers and Hammerstein's musical *Cinderella*. She currently hosts *NickMom Night Out* on Nickelodeon.

ALTHOUGH I DISTINCTLY REMEMBER my favorite teachers, collectively my teachers inspired me to become one myself. Passing on my love of learning, I felt, would help prepare young people to chase their dreams. And so I became a teacher — the worst teacher in the world. My students are either in therapy or writing their memoirs about surviving Ms. Peters's fifth-grade class.

What I didn't understand during that horrendous year I taught was how demanding a teacher's job is. Not only was I required to plan detailed lessons for every subject, but I also needed to adapt each lesson to a student's particular learning style: visual, audio, experiential, and so on. (Many students fell through the cracks because I never did figure out what "and so on" was.)

A teacher needs the social skills to collaborate not just with students but with administrators, parents, and other teachers. Put a room full of adults in a room to discuss anything, and it's a blood sport. The pressure to raise the performance level of your students and your school based on ever-changing educational goals is a Herculean task.

Teachers who can jump through all the hoops and still manage to inspire students to learn and keep on learning are my heroes. I look at them and think, Teaching is more than passing on knowledge. It's a true calling.

JULIE PETERS is an American author of young adult fiction. She has published twenty works, mostly novels, geared toward children and adolescents, many of which deal with LGBT issues. Peters's books have been published in numerous countries in addition to the United States, including South Korea, China, Croatia, Germany, France, Italy, Indonesia, Turkey, and Brazil. Her book *Luna* (2004) was the first young adult novel with a transgender character to be released by a mainstream publisher.

MY FAVORITE TEACHER was Mrs. Lane. I had the pleasure of having her as my teacher in both the fifth and sixth grade. Both my older brothers had Mrs. Lane as their teacher as well. They would come home from school with great stories of what they learned in her class and what a great teacher she was, so needless to say, I was thrilled to finally be a part of her classroom once I was old enough.

What made her a great teacher was her interactions with the students. She made every one of us feel important in our own way. She took an active interest in our lives and made a point of asking us about things we did outside school, such as our music lessons and athletic pursuits. She could often be found at our junior high and high school swim meets, football games, and soccer games, cheering on her former students.

Her teaching style made class fun. Everything was hands-on and interesting. Every day in class brought something new and fun, and she even made our boring math homework and tests seem not so drab. Not surprisingly, the thing I remember most about her was her smile — it never seemed to go away.

Most important, Mrs. Lane taught me — through example and encouragement — that I could do and be anything I wanted. Although she didn't know a thing about the sport of swimming, she took me seriously when I told her in fifth grade that I was going to be an Olympic swimmer. From that day on, she encouraged me to practice and do my best, even if it meant that I would have to leave early from one of her many field trips to make it to my afternoon swim practice.

Mrs. Lane celebrated with my family and friends when I returned home from my first Olympic Games with three gold medals. Her positive attitude and encouragement helped me win those medals, which I did when I was still in high school.

I give a lot of credit to Mrs. Lane and will be thrilled if my daughter is fortunate enough to have a teacher just like her one day.

JANET EVANS won three gold medals for swimming during the 1988 Seoul Olympics. She added to her medal count during the 1992 Barcelona Olympics, winning gold in the 800m and silver in the 400m. Evans participated in the 1996 Olympics but cites running with the Olympic torch as the highlight of that competition.

[Thank You, Teacher]

GREGORY MAGUIRE
author

VINCENTIAN INSTITUTE, CCD (CHILD CULTURAL DIVISION)
Albany, New York

WHEN, ABOUT TWENTY YEARS AGO, I wanted to write a book for fourth- or fifth-grade kids about a pair of clubs in a classroom, one populated by the boys in the room and the other by the girls, it seemed a perfect opportunity to set up a teacher at the head of the classroom as a model of justice, restraint, and wisdom. I had always objected to the depiction of teachers in novels for children as all too often buffoons, sadists, selfish. Most kids I knew in grade school and into middle school loved and admired their teachers.

So I got the chance to create a teacher filled with her own peculiarities, as all teachers are — she was still grieving over the accidental death of her fiancé, who was run over by a float at the Macy's Thanksgiving Day Parade. She drove a motorcycle and lived with her mother, who ran a bakery and an auto repair shop. Her name was Miss Earth, Miss Germaine Earth.

The series — called The Hamlet Chronicles — followed the children through a cycle of seven holidays in a single school year: Halloween, Thanksgiving, Christmas, Valentine's Day, Easter, April Fool's, and Fourth of July. In these books, the teacher is a steady presence. Indeed, the crisis at the end of the first novel is that the teacher is bitten by a Siberian tarantula, and the children must relinquish memberships in their clubs to come together to save her. The novel ends with the first graders rather than Our Heroes winning the first prize at the Halloween pageant:

> The first prize in the Hallowe'en Pageant of Horrors went to the kindergartners dressed as seventeen blind mice. "Well, they were sweet," said Miss Earth, telling her class the news. "But in a way I wished that my class had won it, for I was proud of how you worked together on that skit at the last minute. Neither Tattletales nor Copycats." She looked at them with the quiet satisfaction of a true teacher getting the job done. "Maybe you're learning a little something after all."
>
> "We worked together to save your life!" said Pearl Hotchkiss.
>
> "There's no prize for that, alas," said Miss Earth.
>
> But her students, gazing fondly at her, knew she was wrong. The first prize was right there in front of them.

It is this sort of devotion that students rightly feel for the teachers who change their lives. We all have benefited from such teachers, and some of us have been willing to stand up and do the same for the young today. Blessings on all such good souls, I say.

GREGORY MAGUIRE is the author of nearly forty books for adults and young people, including the Boston Globe-Horn Book Honor Book *Egg & Spoon*, and the novel *Wicked*, which inspired the Broadway musical by the same name. A well-known public speaker and reviewer for the Sunday *New York Times*, Maguire has also written and performed original work for *All Things Considered*.

[Unforgettable]

JOAN BAKER
voice-over actress

MRS. REAMER
fifth grade, Nova Albion Elementary School, Terra Linda, California

MY FIFTH-GRADE YEAR IN SCHOOL was by far the best I had experienced since kindergarten. It was all because of my teacher, Mrs. Reamer. She was truly unforgettable. That style, that face, and that warm, wonderful smile became my refuge after four years of educational turmoil.

I grew up in Marin County in the early '60s as a biracial child. Racism was still rampant, and liberals were just beginning to figure out how best to position themselves for maximum political correctness. The politics of race was in flux. It was all still new, and not much from the progressive side of things had filtered down in the way of racial sensitivity in the predominantly white schools like mine. Being biracial made the whole experience that much more psychedelic. I felt like I didn't fit in, even though I didn't know what it was about me that was creating my isolation.

Biracialism was confusing and frightening, even to adults. They didn't seem to know how to include me in the grand social scheme. The very few blacks that were around didn't accept me as black, and the whites didn't accept me as white. And no one accepted biracial as a category.

As a result, I was very wary of putting myself out there, while at the same time wanting to be liked by all. I was shy on the one hand and very outgoing on the other. Naturally, this preoccupation with fitting in made it difficult for me to focus in school. My grades suffered, and that brought on even more negative attention. In one case, my teacher literally sat me in the back of the classroom with a dunce cap on my head. I was crushed. But fortunately I had a certain spunk that kept me fighting for my piece of happiness. As I entered each new grade, I felt as if I had to start all over again trying to win my teacher over — trying to prove I was capable, lovable, and worthy.

Enter Mrs. Reamer. She greeted me with a smile every morning. She laughed at my jokes and loved to listen to my tales of woe. She treated me as if I was her own — loved and adored.

Her approach to education was special. As a class we painted cardboard boxes (in the '60s style of art) and used them to partition a room into our personal reading lounge. There, in our own space, Mrs. Reamer would gently encourage and guide us. By the fifth grade, I was gun-shy about reading in front of others. God knows I didn't want to wear another dunce cap. Mrs. Reamer worked with me one-on-one in our private reading room until I developed my skills and courage. By the end of the school year, I could stand in front of the class and read without a fear in the world.

I was so inspired by Mrs. Reamer that at the end of fifth grade, I wanted to do something to show my appreciation. I had overheard a conversation she had with another teacher about her love of bike riding, so I started collecting money to buy her a ten-speed bike. I went door-to-door to the homes of every student in our class to collect enough money. Then my dad drove me to a bike store, where I picked out a bright-orange ten-speed.

I can still see the smile on her face as she road her bike around the school yard while we kids screamed at the top of our lungs. But here's the clincher. I arrived late for school on the day her gift was presented, so Mrs. Reamer never got to know that I was the mastermind behind her newfound happiness. She never knew that I loved her for what she had given me. This missing link troubled me for years. It is only through the opportunity to share this story today that I feel redeemed. I want to tell all the Mrs. Reamers of the world the magical power you possess in your roles as teachers, nurturers, givers of life. Unforgettable.

JOAN BAKER is the author of *Secrets of Voice-over Success*, cocreator and cohost of That's Voiceover! career expo, cowriter of a monthly advice voice-over column for *Backstage* magazine, and cofounder of the newly formed Society of Voice Arts and Sciences, which oversees the Voice Art Awards. She is active on the teaching circuit, engaging students on a visceral level to personally connect with the craft and trends of commercial advertising scripts. Baker is also one of New York's premier voice-over actors. Her professional voice-over credits include narrating a documentary about the founding of the William Jefferson Clinton Library, now a part of the library's permanent display; the Academy of Television; ABC Daytime; ESPN; Showtime; Chase Bank; American Express; the Academy of Television Arts and Sciences; and many more. Baker received the 2014 V.O.I.C.E. Community Award for Outstanding Service.

[I Met Her Only Once]

RUDY GASKINS
producer

MS. PARKER
substitute teacher, Bunker Hill Elementary, Washington, DC

MY FAVORITE TEACHER was actually a substitute teacher whom I met only once. Her name was Ms. Parker. Most students tend to coast when there's a substitute teacher, I suppose because they assume these teachers may be less committed or less informed and that they may even see themselves as unable to have a significant impact in a single day, perhaps never to see the same students ever again. And trust me, our class was gleeful to hear that we would be having a substitute, until we heard it was Ms. Parker. You see, Ms. Parker had a school-wide reputation for being as strict as they come. I had never experienced her, but the word was out in a big way that Ms. Parker was the last teacher you ever wanted to have as a substitute. And when you're in the fourth grade, "strict" means you could be eaten alive for misbehaving. So I decided that the only way to avoid this woman's wrath was to be a perfect student. Mind you, I wasn't a perfect student even with my regular teacher — far from it. But that was not the case on this fateful occasion. I made up my mind that I would not be called out, I would not be sent to the principal's office, I would not be sent home with a note pinned to my shirt, and I would not be put to stand in the corner during class. But most of all, I would not be swallowed whole by a dragon lady.

Because I was in such an attentive space from which to receive Ms. Parker, I discovered something that changed my life. Ms. Parker wanted to focus on English grammar that day. And as much as I felt challenged by English grammar, I felt I needed to rise to the occasion. So I listened in a way that only the fear of a dragon lady can cause you to listen. And I heard, for the first time, how wonderfully magical language could be. And I saw that the dragon lady was actually one of the most loving and giving human beings a student or parent or school could ever hope for. She turned me upside down in one day and gave me a love for learning. In my mind the dragon became a butterfly, but the transformation occurred within me. She cared with all her heart about teaching, and she drank in my attentiveness, careful not to lose a moment of opportunity to fill me up with all she had. I believe she tossed one or two children out of the classroom and sent them marching off to the principal's office, but she and I became fast partners in learning. I literally fell in love; I couldn't get enough and longed for her to return to take over my classroom forever.

I never saw Ms. Parker again. And I never forgot her, either.

RUDY GASKINS is an Emmy Award–winning creative director and branding expert. In 2001, after holding executive roles at Court TV and the Food Network, he launched Push Creative Advertising, a full-service branding agency providing strategic marketing, graphic design, and video/film production. His accounts include American Express, the Tribeca Film Festival, Lexus, and BET. Gaskins has written, produced, and directed hundreds of commercials, promos, and marketing campaigns and has directed documentaries for PBS. Gaskins and his wife, Joan Baker, are the cofounders of That's Voiceover!, an annual career expo, and the creators of the newly formed Society of Voice Arts and Sciences and the Voice Arts Awards.

WHAT I REMEMBER — second grade and walking through the door that joined our class with Mrs. Cameron's class. What I was afraid of — Bobby Bennett and his squinting eyes. We were trying something new at our elementary school — electives for second graders. Without even needing to think about it, I signed up for creative writing.

What I remember — the fat-lined beige paper and the blank space to draw a picture. What I was afraid of — I had nothing interesting to write or say. We were told to write a story about a favorite animal, to leave nothing out.

What I remember — I chose a giraffe, I'm guessing because I am tall. What I was afraid of — that my story would not be liked by Mrs. Cameron, a teacher I didn't know. I ignored the rules and included not only a giraffe in my story but also a crocodile and a dachshund. I drew purple cheetah spots on my giraffe so it couldn't be ignored.

What I remember — Mrs. Cameron coming up to me as

I went back to my regular classroom. What I was afraid of —
that she would say I did it wrong, that my story was no good.
I could see Bobby Bennett behind her, squinting his eyes and
rubbing his hands together as if I was done for, all washed up.

What I remember — Mrs. Cameron bending down so we
were at eye level to tell me, "I loved your story. You have the
makings of a writer. You could grow up to be an author if you
chose." What I was afraid of — that I'd someday forget she
said this, the faith she had in me at such a young age. Thirty-
six years and four published books later, her belief in me still
stays.

KELLI RUSSELL AGODON is the author of *Letters from the Emily Dickin-
son Room* (2010), winner of the ForeWord Magazine Poetry Book of the
Year Award and a finalist for the Washington State Book Awards. She
is also the author of *Small Knots* and the chapbook *Geography*. Agodon
coedited the first ebook anthology of contemporary women's poetry,
Fire on Her Tongue, and was the editor of *Crab Creek Review* and the
cofounder of Two Sylvias Press. Her third book of poems, *Hourglass
Museum*, was published in 2014. She is also working on a memoir entitled *Retreat*.

CAROL MUSKE-DUKES
poet and novelist

SISTER JEANNE D'ARC
first grade, Holy Spirit School, St. Paul, Minnesota

HER NAME WAS SISTER JEANNE D'ARC, but to us — her twenty or so first graders at Holy Spirit School in St. Paul, Minnesota, in the fifties — she was Sister John Dark. It was not a frightening name to us, because we were quite new to words, aware of their power yet often unsure of their meaning. We were illiterate and so the sounds of words meant more than symbols we could not yet decipher. Voice and presence were everything to us — and Sister John Dark's voice and presence were light filled. Her voice was musical, and her face and form, even in her starched black-and-white habit, radiated a brightness, a tenderness. She loved us; we felt that.

Her love, as a teacher of children who could not yet read, was pedagogical power. Her love took the terror out of the unknown, the strange symbols on the page. We learned phonics, we sounded words out, but it was her hand pointing at a word as we struggled with utterance — T-R-E-E — that provided the dawning breakthrough.

I remember bringing her purple and white lilacs, swaddled in damp gauze, from the wildly fragrant bushes in our yard. I remember her hand hovering as she traced the letters for me, as I made sounds. I remember the exact moment when suddenly, as I mouthed the letters — T-R-E-E — I looked up, and in a flash I saw the tree outside the classroom window and the TREE on the page and understood that the word "meant" the trunk and the branches with green leaves moving in the breeze — TREE! Suddenly, I could read — and then, suddenly, I could write! I read books and I wrote stories for Sister John Dark. I wrote about a princess trapped inside a F-L-O-W-E-R who also fought in a W-A-R. Sister John Dark gave me inspiration, and I knew I would be inspired as long as I lived. Books! The library! Reading and writing poems! Later, when I came to understand the history (and spelling) of her name, I sometimes conflated my memory of her shining presence with an image of her heroic French namesake, Jeanne d'Arc.

As I grew up, as I entered high school, college, and grad school — as I became a writer and a teacher myself — I never forgot her. I wrote a poem I dedicated to her, about bringing the lilacs to school to place in her hands — that I included in one of my poetry collections.

Many years later I was visiting my family in Minnesota and heard from a longtime friend with whom I'd gone to grade school that Sister John Dark was still around — that she'd left the convent and married a former priest and was now a political activist in the Twin Cities. She had another name now, an "ordinary" name — and my friend knew how to locate her and planned to look her up.

On another visit to Minnesota, not long afterward, I was invited to give a poetry reading at the University of Minnesota. I heard from a group of my grade school and high school friends, who were attending the reading, that they would be bringing Sister John Dark, now in her eighties.

Suddenly, there she was. She walked in with my friends before the reading began — now an elderly woman but with a bright vibrant face that stirred my memory. She smiled at me, and we embraced. I had no lilacs to give her, but I gave her another gift. I dedicated my poetry reading to her and I thanked her for all that she had done for me. She'd taken my hand, she'd led me into the kingdom of literacy, I said. She'd given me my love of words — and now I could thank her in the words of the poem I'd written for her. I could read that poem aloud to her, and to the assembled audience that day, because on another day, fifty years earlier, a young nun named Sister John Dark had taught me how.

CAROL MUSKE-DUKES is the author of eight books of poems, four novels, and two essay collections. She is a professor of English and creative writing at the University of Southern California and a former poet laureate of California. A National Book Award and Los Angeles Times Book Prize finalist, she has also been the recipient of the Pushcart Prize, among many other honors. In addition, many of her books have been New York Times Notable Books. She writes and reviews for the Los Angeles Times, the New York Times, the Huffington Post, and the New Yorker "Page-Turner." She recently wrote a play entitled I Married the Icepick Killer. For more, see www.carolmuskedukes.com.

[Teachers]

C. K. WILLIAMS
poet

MISS WALZER
sixth grade

I.

The more than mere fervor with which our teacher,
Miss Walzer, pointed out to our clearly to her
depressingly homogeneous sixth grade,
that not only were negroes, "black" people, not black,
but that we weren't the color white, either,
came to me last night as I watched on PBS
the newly arrived "white" principal of a failing
mostly minority inner-city school
who'd left his job in a suburb and taken a pay cut
to be a "turnaround education specialist" here.
Sympathetic, well-intentioned, experienced,
(or so he'd thought — "I wasn't prepared," he admitted,
"for the pandemonium at the metal detector")
his tenure, for all his past the-call-of-duty diligence,
had so far shown few results —
the general sense of chaos was undiminished,

the teachers as dispirited as ever,
and now his supervisors from the Board of Ed
are telling him his "remediation recovery plan"
isn't going well; test scores are off.
He looks — I doubt he'd want to hear this —
ready to give it up. With the meeting barely over,
another of the seemingly unending fights
has broken out in the corridor,
and he asks the film crew to stop.

2.

When I download the transcript of that program,
I'm struck by how often the words *respect*
and *disrespect* occur, as in "He disrespected me,"
or "These children don't have respect for themselves,
so they're not going to have respect for me..."
Repeated and repeated, it becomes like a communal wail:
for the principal, it's "the basis of understanding,"
for the teachers it means having their students stay awake,
not talk back or throw books or chairs —
("They won't run me out of here," says one) —
and for the children, the most troubled and disruptive,
who'll barely permit themselves to glance at an adult,
it seems the very ground of their defiance —
they're like soldiers in some moral war
that only they comprehend is under way.
In a blurry still, a boy, ten or so,
in T-shirt to his knees and sneaks,
head bowed, is being led away by a guard.
Insolence, violence, policemen —
what would generous Miss Walzer have thought?
When she said that thing about our whiteness,

she'd made perfectly clear what she'd meant:
that we believed we were better for being alike,
that we were already contaminated by disdain,
and though we didn't know it, our souls were at risk.

3.
"No more pencils, no more books" — is that
still sung the last day of school before summer?
"No more teacher's dirty looks..." I'd forgotten that.
Did we ever mean Miss Walzer by that,
whom I think back on with such esteem?
I used to imagine her admirable wisdom
would magically migrate from her brain to mine,
but I was an indifferent student; I fidgeted,
daydreamed, didn't do my homework, didn't,
as my teachers often said, apply myself.
I wonder if that bewildering term is still in use,
if that principal, so thwarted and besieged,
would ever have occasion to use it?
Not likely: he looks utterly,
wearily out of things to say.
Is anyone not? Does anyone know, though,
who to blame for this, or even what
to blame them for? Never mind blame,
or fault, or shame: how to feel other than regret
for so much lost, so much left unlearned?
Come dusk, the classrooms emptied,
the books shut tight, those forsaken treasures
of knowledge must batter the fading blackboards
and swarm the silent, sleeping halls,
like shades of lives never to be lived.

C. K. WILLIAMS (1936–2015) won the Pulitzer Prize, the National Book Award, and the National Book Critics Circle Award, among many other honors. He has published several poetry collections: *Wait*, *Writers Writing Dying*, *All at Once*, and *Selected Later Poems*. In addition, he has published a critical study, *On Whitman*, and a book of essays, *In Time: Poets, Poems, and the Rest*. Williams was a member of the American Academy of Arts and Letters.

┌───┐
│   │
│   [Suzanne Will Be a Writer]   │
│   │
│   SUZANNE HARPER   │
│   author   │
│   │
│   MRS. WINSTON   │
│   second grade, Friendswood Elementary, Friendswood, Texas │
│   │
└───┘

WHEN I WAS IN THE FIRST GRADE, I didn't like to read. Not at all. The mere thought of picking up one of my first-grade readers made me fidget.

See Dick run? See Jane climb a tree? See Spot chase a ball? Could the people who created these textbooks make reading any more boring?

Then, in the summer between first and second grade, my mother took my sister and me to the local five-and-dime store. We could each buy a book of our own, she said. Any book. Our choice.

I picked a Bobbsey Twins book because my sister and I are twins. It was (as I later realized) a mass-produced series churned out by a legion of low-paid ghost writers. But for me, it was a revelation.

I remember starting to read the book and not stopping until I had to go to bed. I remember waking up the next morning and finishing the book over breakfast. And I distinctly recall reading the last page, closing the book, and thinking: I want to do that when I grow up. I want to be a writer.

So I entered Mrs. Winston's second-grade class that fall an avid reader. I'm not sure if I told her that I wanted to write books, but I clearly loved to read and talk about stories. A few months after the start of the year, my mother attended a parent-teacher conference. During their talk, Mrs. Winston said to my mother, "Suzanne *will* be a writer."

Of course, my mother passed this on to me.

Looking back, I think this might have been a rather casual comment, but I took it as prophecy. The matter was settled. I wasn't just hoping and wishing to be a writer. I was going to be a writer. Mrs. Winston had said so.

I wanted to prove myself to her, so I kept reading (making long lists of every book I read) and writing. I even organized some friends to create a small book of poems and short stories, which we gave to Mrs. Winston as an end-of-the-school-year present.

In the years that followed, I stayed on that path: taking workshops; entering writing competitions; earning college degrees in journalism, English, and creative writing; and trying my hand at mystery novels and picture books and screenplays in night classes after college.

Finally, several decades after I read that first Bobbsey Twins book, I published my own novel.

To some people, it may seem like an overstatement to say that one offhand comment when I was seven years old set my life's direction, but not to me. That quiet vote of confidence made me feel that I already was a writer — all I had to do was put in the work to make it happen.

That's my story, but as I was thinking about it, I began to wonder if other people had the same experience. We often hear stories about adults who crush kids' dreams with an ill-timed, sarcastic, or even cruel comment. What about the opposite? I decided to ask my friends and colleagues if they had any stories to share, either their own or someone else's. I found out that there are a lot of Mrs. Winstons out there.

Here are some of the stories I heard:

A sixteen-year-old girl was failing her journalism class until her teacher found out she was also enrolled in photography. The teacher asked her to take a photograph to run with another student's story. It was a good photo. The teacher told her so and asked her to be the class's staff photographer (a position that didn't exist). That was all the student needed. She made the role of staff photographer her own, blossomed into an A student, and went on to have a successful photography career.

A writing teacher had a student with learning disabilities who never turned in any assignments. He did talk a lot in class, however — and he always talked about food and restaurants. The teacher casually suggested that he write food reviews. Immediately, he began turning in assignments that were so good they actually shocked his teacher.

A middle-school boy always tried out for plays because his best friend liked to act. However, he rarely got roles because he was so quiet. One day, after he helped fix a classroom computer, his theater teacher told the class, "He's our tech wizard!" That was all the encouragement he needed to join the technical crew, where he found that his real talent was behind the scenes, working on the lighting and sound.

I know there are thousands of other stories like these being enacted every day at schools across the country. I'm grateful to Mrs. Winston for the words she was moved to say all those years ago and for the words that have filled my life ever since.

SUZANNE HARPER is the author of two young adult novels, *The Secret Life of Sparrow Delaney* and *The Juliet Club*; a middle-grade series, The Unseen World of Poppy Malone; and several nonfiction books, *The Real Spy's Guide to Becoming a Spy*, *33 More Things Every Girl Should Know*, and more. Please visit her website at www.suzanneharper.com or read her blog at www.sharperauthor.wordpress.com.

┌───┐
│   │
│   [It Only Took Me a Moment   │
│   or Two to Recognize Him]   │
│   │
│   PETER SELGIN   │
│   author and playwright   │
│   │
│   │
│   MR. FESH   │
│   sixth grade, Frank M. Berry Elementary, Bethel, Connecticut │
│   │
└───┘

NOT LONG AGO I did a reading at a Barnes & Noble bookstore in Danbury, Connecticut, a few miles from the town where I grew up and lived for eighteen years. It was a beautiful autumn day, sunny, breezy, and cool (as the forecasters like to say). On the drive up from the Bronx my companion and I marveled at the fiery displays of colors in the trees along the Saw Mill Parkway. This is my favorite time of year, when the leaves begin to fall, when the sky rains dry flecks of yellow, and the earth wears a bright-colored quilt of red and golden leaves. I wondered, on such a beautiful day, who would want to spend an hour indoors listening to someone read from a book?

To my surprise quite a few people, many of them strangers, and many more familiar. My proud mother invited many of her friends, and there were faces I recognized from my undergraduate year at Western Connecticut State University, and even a few faces of people I'd gone to high school with in Bethel. One friend, Mark, had driven down from Vermont with his new family, a beautiful wife and two equally beautiful boys, one still at his mother's breast. Mark and I had been in touch but hadn't seen each other in years. Mark looked good — a little huskier, his hair gone completely white, but otherwise unchanged, and with a smile that spoke eloquently of the pleasures of fatherhood and family.

But of all the faces both familiar and unfamiliar, one touched me more deeply than any other. I was speaking to Mark's wife when I looked up and saw a man approaching. He wore a white Windbreaker and a baseball cap — Yankees, I think. He was tall, broad shouldered. It took me only a moment or two to recognize him, despite his being out of the narrow focal range of my nearsighted eyes; and even after I had recognized him, still there was a moment of confusion, since I was unprepared to believe what my eyes told me and what seemed a little too much like a dream. For here was my sixth-grade teacher, Mr. Fesh, come to check on his pupil.

"I know this man," I said out loud as he approached, a smile already spreading across my face.

In forty years he hadn't changed that much. He was still tall, still good-looking (from what I could see under the shadowy visor of the baseball cap). I recognized his deep voice. "Mr. Selgin," he said — the same form of address he had used in sixth grade. I didn't say, "Mr. Fesh!" I didn't have to; my smile spoke for me.

We shook hands, but that wouldn't do: I had to give him a hug.

In sixth grade I had a crush on Mr. Fesh. Not a homosexual crush, since I liked girls in that way, but the crush of a sixth grader ripe for role models. My father, after all, was much older than most fathers I knew, and though he had other virtues and charms and I loved him dearly, I found him lacking in certain physical respects (he detested all sports and refused to jump into water). And here was this teacher, a man — the first male teacher I'd ever had — handsome, tall (my father was handsome but already gray, half-bald, with a paunch, and not tall), scarcely twenty-four years old. He looked like Paul Newman.

Back in sixth grade Mr. Fesh still had all his hair. He didn't need the baseball cap. He wore spiffy blazers, pale blue and yellow oxford cloth shirts, and sharp striped neckties with silver and gold tie pins. I remember going to the local Caldor department store and searching among the racks for ties and blazers like the ones Mr. Fesh wore, and gleaming tie pins to go with them. I had no reason to wear such garments and no events to wear them to. Still, I prized them because I wanted to be like Mr. Fesh. He wore shiny brown wing tips. I begged my mother for a pair. Wing tips!

Mr. Fesh must have known that I had a crush on him — a teacher's pet crush. I suspect he liked it. I'm a teacher now myself and wouldn't mind thinking that one or two of my students had crushes on me, though I don't imagine that any of them do. They are older undergraduates, and children of a more (with good reason) skeptical generation, and much less inclined to hero-worship their teachers.

Once my mother invited Mr. Fesh and his wife for dinner. What an exciting night! It was like having all four of the Beatles over for supper. I remember little about that evening beyond my excitement. Mr. Fesh drove a spiffy red convertible Mustang: the perfect car for a pubescent boy's role model. I remember watching through the window and seeing it come up the driveway. I remember the feeling that accompanied this spectacle, the sense that anything could happen, that miracles really did exist in this world.

After teaching sixth grade for a year or two, Mr. Fesh became a phys ed instructor. One of his sons had a brief baseball career and played in the major leagues for several seasons until an injury of some sort cut his career short. I imagine that this must have been a huge blow to his father. Mr. Fesh, meanwhile, went on to become a baseball scout. I learned these things over the years through the grapevine.

Now here was Mr. Fesh, alive and looking well. Retired, he told me. I asked him if he planned to stay for the reading. "Nah." He shook his head. "Don't think so. Too boring." I recognized that glint in his eye and his deadpan delivery. "Now *there's* someone I need to say hello to," he said, and I followed his eyes to my eighty-year-old mother. I remembered how he and my mom had flirted with each other, how a few times on school field trips they sat together on the bus until someone warned Mr. Fesh, "You better stop sitting next to that lady; people are starting to talk." It seems my mother and I both had a crush on my sixth-grade teacher.

While reading to my small audience, I saw no sign of Mr. Fesh. Perhaps he had left after all, I thought. But as soon as I'd finished he appeared again, off to the side, giving me the thumbs-up.

"I'm proud of you," he said. Had my dead father come back as a ghost and uttered those same words, I would not have been more pleased.

Over the years I've often wondered if it's all been worth it — the rejection, the struggle, the disappointments and despair and disillusionment that come with a vocation in the arts, if they have served any real purpose, if there's been a meaning to what I've done, or tried to do, with my life for the past thirty years. Most of all I've wondered if the sacrifices (money, sound sleep, security) have been worth it. Yesterday afternoon, when

Mr. Fesh gave me the thumbs-up, I had my answer: a resounding yes.

Sometimes, if only for a moment or two, here and there, life really does mean something.

Thanks, Mr. Fesh.

PETER SELGIN is the author of a story collection, *Drowning Lessons*, winner of the 2007 Flannery O'Connor Award for Fiction; two novels, *Life Goes to the Movies* and *The Water Master*, which won the Pirate's Alley/Faulkner Society Prize; several books on the craft of fiction; and numerous children's books. In addition, one of his two memoirs, *Confessions of a Left-Handed Man: An Artist's Memoir*, was short-listed for the William Saroyan International Prize for Writing. His essay "The Kuhreihen Melody" won the Missouri Review Jeffrey E. Smith Editors' Prize, the Dana Award for the Essay, and a Pushcart nomination from Wally Lamb. Selgin teaches at Antioch University's low-residency MFA program and is an assistant professor of creative writing at Georgia College & State University.

MEG WOLITZER
author

MRS. GERBE
first grade, South Woods Elementary School, Syosset, New York

I HAVE A THEORY that in the beginning, writers often write for someone in particular. This someone may be a parent, a best friend, a person they've never met, or it may be a teacher. When I was in first grade I had a wonderful, lively, exciting teacher named Mrs. Gerbe, and once a week or so, when the classroom was otherwise quiet, she would invite me up to her desk to dictate short stories to her. She'd write them down as fast as I could tell them, and I sort of felt like the executive of a company giving dictation to a secretary. ("Take a letter, Mrs. Gerbe.") My first-grade handwriting was tortured and slow (not all that different from my middle-aged handwriting), and my teacher knew it, but I was imaginative, which she also knew. And so while the other kids were doing something dull, like napping, or guzzling those containers of sugared orange drinks that we all mainlined during the 1960s and 1970s, there I was, stationed at Mrs. Gerbe's big desk, pacing back and forth and letting the ideas come.

Early on, my stories were about subjects I knew absolutely nothing about. (I know this because my mother, a writer, who was also an enormous inspiration to me, saved them all, and I do mean all.) One story that I wrote for Mrs. Gerbe was about two truck drivers. It seemed really sophisticated to me at the time, really grown-up, to write about the world of these tough men. I believe the dialogue between the truck drivers went something like, "Get up on the rig, Mack." I didn't even know what a rig *was*. But it sounded good; it sounded like life. I wanted to impress Mrs. Gerbe with my knowledge of the adult world that seemed to loom large all around me, a world I hadn't yet joined. I really had no idea of what that world actually consisted of. But a very kind teacher who believed in my abilities allowed me to fantasize a little bit about things that were outside my own sphere, and though I imagined I was primarily impressing her, I now think I was forging my identity as a writer, creating myself through my own childlike images and words, facilitated by the adult hand of a caring and skillful teacher.

In the class photograph from first grade, Mrs. Gerbe is wearing one of those dresses with a complicated, tied collar, which many teachers seemed to wear back then. She is also smiling with an expression of contentment. I feel pretty confident that she loved her work, took pleasure in the imaginations of the small students who bobbed and skipped around her. In creating a classroom in which imagination was respected and encouraged, she set off various bottle rockets in the brains of her students; certainly she set off one in mine. Many years after first grade, I returned to give a reading at a bookstore in a town not far from where I had gone to elementary school, and I invited Mrs. Gerbe, and she came. Though the rest of the evening was festive and full, seeing her was the highlight for me. I wanted her to know how much it had meant to me to have her as my first-grade teacher, my caring guide through learning, and, meaningfully, as my own personal secretary.

MEG WOLITZER's novels include *The Interestings*, *The Uncoupling*, *The Ten-Year Nap*, *The Position*, and *The Wife*. She is also the author of a novel for middle-grade readers, *The Fingertips of Duncan Dorfman*, and a novel for young adults, *Belzhar*. Wolitzer's short fiction has appeared in *The Best American Short Stories* and *The Pushcart Prize*. A faculty member of the MFA program at Stony Brook Southampton, she was a guest artist in the Princeton Atelier program at Princeton University in September 2013, along with singer-songwriter Suzzy Roche.

[PART TWO]

Middle School

[He Could Understand]

KATHERINE MARSH
author

MR. HUBNER
English, Fieldston School, Bronx, New York

TWENTY-FIVE YEARS AGO, on my first day of seventh grade, I walked into my assigned English class to discover a strange sight. A middle-aged man with thinning blond hair was sitting behind the teacher's desk puffing away on a piece of chalk. Immediately two things were clear to me: (1) He was dying for a smoke, and (2) He wasn't bothering to hide this from a roomful of seventh graders. This made him the most interesting teacher I'd had all day.

All day long, I'd been meeting my teachers — some were strict, others more laidback — but all of them seemed generally colorless the way most adults seem to kids. It was impossible to imagine any of them feeling the heights of anger or despair I felt daily over my parents' ongoing divorce, of feeling powerless or alone or different. But this man smoking his chalk seemed like maybe, just maybe, he could understand.

His name was Mr. Hubner and he would be my English teacher for both seventh and ninth grades. He would introduce me to Eudora Welty and William Faulkner, to James Baldwin and the blues, to Holden Caulfield and Hamlet. He would be the first openly gay adult in my life. He was also openly sarcastic (mostly at the expense of lazy students), openly grumpy (he was constantly trying to quit smoking), and openly critical (not only of our essays, which he picked apart in class, but of the books we were assigned to read).

But when he taught his favorite writers, the ones whose photos he enshrined on the back wall of his classroom, he gave the sense that he was sharing something deeply personal, something that could stem the flood of alienation and pain that came with growing up.

There are teachers who teach you how to read, and then there are teachers who teach you how to find yourself through reading. It was no coincidence that I was in Mr. Hubner's class when I decided to become a writer. It was ninth grade and my parents' divorce was finally reaching its bitter end. I had stopped talking to my father and had moments when I fantasized about being dead. In the midst of this, Mr. Hubner assigned us a lengthy report on an artist of our choosing. At first, I figured I would pick John Steinbeck, my favorite writer, whose dust bowl novels reflected my own bleak mood. But Mr. Hubner, who preferred the Southern novelists, nudged me toward Flannery O'Connor instead.

I still remember writing that report, the tower of O'Connor themed books stacked up beside my old Macintosh, the photos of peacocks (O'Connor's favorite animal), which I assembled to decorate the cover. As it turned out, O'Connor was a wonderful antidote to adolescent misery. She was deeply eccentric and undeniably tragic (she would die at age 39 of lupus) but unapologetic and sharp-tongued. "You shall know the truth, and the truth shall make you odd," she wrote. "Anybody who has survived his childhood has enough information about life to last him the rest of his days."

In short, she felt very much like a fellow traveler. As I meticulously wrote that report, I realized that my life too — the difficult parts, especially — wasn't meaningless. It was material.

What a writer, especially a young one, needs most is an appreciative audience. Mr. Hubner could be critical and grumpy but his praise, when it came, was genuine and effusive. Long before I ever received a positive review as a novelist, I still remember the heart-thumping thrill I felt when Mr. Hubner returned that Flannery O'Connor report. The A-plus on the back wasn't just a grade; it was a validation. I was a writer. And I was going to be okay.

KATHERINE MARSH is the Edgar Award–winning children's author of *The Night Tourist*; *The Twilight Prisoner*; *Jepp, Who Defied the Stars*; and *The Door by the Staircase*. She lives with her family in Brussels, Belgium. You can learn more about her at www.katherinemarsh.com.

[As Tall as I Would Ever Need to Be]

ROBERT REICH
political economist

BILL JAVANE
sixth grade, Lewisboro School, South Salem, New York

AT THE AGE OF ELEVEN I entered Bill Javane's sixth grade — short, timid, anxious about almost everything a preadolescent can be anxious about. In the course of the following ten months he opened my eyes to the world and to my own powers in that world, and in so doing he not only eased my anxieties and timidity but also allowed me to feel I was as tall as I would ever need to be. I recall him as a middle-aged man (in fact, he could have been in his thirties) with a black mustache, curly black hair, a warm smile, and a playfulness that made everything he talked about in that classroom alive with possibility. On one occasion he pointed out the pretensions of white missionaries in sub-Saharan Africa who tried to dress tribal women in cotton dresses that hid their breasts, only to return later to find the women still wearing the dresses but with large holes cut out so they could feed their babies and stay cool. On another he talked about why civilizations have needed to believe in God. On another he explained why scientific advances are usually little more than simpler explanations for new data. I remember him reading the *Odyssey* to the class and weeping at the call of the sirens. I think I wept too. Bill Javane turned teaching into an inspiration, and inspiration into imagination. Through him I could imagine myself as an adult — seeking to avoid pretension, seeking to believe in forces I could not explain, seeking to explain ever more elegantly what I could understand, seeking to be touched by the stories of eternity. And the adult I imagined became the adult I wanted to be.

ROBERT REICH is a politician, academic, writer, and political commentator. He served as the twenty-second US secretary of labor, serving under President Bill Clinton from 1993 to 1997. He is the cocreator of the award-winning film *Inequality for All*, and his book *Saving Capitalism* was published in 2015.

[She Had Expectations]

ELIZABETH MCCRACKEN
author

MRS. BLOOM
English, F. A. Day Middle School, Newton, Massachusetts

I WAS THAT TERRIBLE THING: a precocious and lazy child. Teachers either hated me (for instance, my fourth-grade teacher, who had me copy pages from the dictionary when I wouldn't shut up in class) or loved me for no good reason (my sixth-grade teacher for some reason allowed me to grade other students' tests). I sassed and I sucked up, alternately — anything, really, to get out of working.

In elementary school I got good grades. Then I went to junior high, and I discovered that a good memory and too much confidence did not actually replace studying. Additionally, my friends were going through puberty, and I was such a late bloomer, I was not even budding. This made me feel as though I were the only sane person in the lunatic asylum, which in turn made me go crazy too. I drew anonymous cartoons of the teachers. I wore costumes instead of my gym costume. My talking back got so bad I was regularly thrown out of class. I wasn't a bad kid, just backward and bored. And then I had Mrs. Bloom for eighth-grade English.

She was, we were told, a widow, and she was young and beautiful, with dark hair and red lipstick. It was her first year at the school, I think. Mrs. Bloom did something very simple for me. It's astonishing that nobody had done it before. She had expectations. She told me that I was a good writer, and she also gave me bad grades. She could tell when I didn't put the time in, and when I did — this astonished me, that a teacher could tell this kind of thing. She told me that talent didn't make any difference if you didn't work. This too was news to me, but I believed her. She was the first teacher whose good opinion of me and my work meant something. Really, she was my first reader — that is, the first person who read my work and wanted it to be *good*. She took me seriously. I changed in her class. She taught me impatience and ambition. I still have a thank-you card she wrote to me at the end of the year.

She left the school soon afterward, and I did too, and I lost track of her, and so did the school. I asked people about her, but she had disappeared. One of the teachers I asked mentioned my teacher's sadness of her young husband's death: she never really got over it. Every now and then I tried to track her down, but Susan Bloom is a common name. Once I even thought I had found her, teaching at a college in Boston, the right age, the right credentials. I squinted at the photograph, and then I wrote. You could tell that the Susan Bloom I wrote to wished she were *my* Susan Bloom, but she wasn't.

About ten years ago I gave an interview to a newspaper from my hometown; the journalist wanted to know about my experience with the public schools. So I talked about Susan Bloom, thinking maybe some news would blow into my email box. Still nothing.

Then, a year and a half ago, she found me.

Her name was now Susan Alport, the name she'd been

born with. She'd read the interview and found my email through my website. She'd left my junior high and become an artist, gone to the Museum School in Boston, and would come to the reading I was giving in my hometown the next week.

There isn't a good story about our meeting, except that it was wonderful and still makes me tear up to think of it. In some ways she wasn't like I remembered (she was shorter; it was more than thirty years later), and yet she was so instantly recognizable to me, so familiar and comforting — *hamish*, you'd say in Yiddish. She looked not like any of my aunts in particular but was auntlike in the way of my mother's family. We embraced. "You haven't changed," she lied, and I thought, Thank heavens that isn't true.

ELIZABETH MCCRACKEN is the author of five books: *Here's Your Hat What's Your Hurry* (stories), the novels *The Giant's House* and *Niagara Falls All Over Again*, the memoir *An Exact Replica of a Figment of My Imagination*, and *Thunderstruck & Other Stories*. She's received grants and fellowships from the Guggenheim Foundation, the National Endowment for the Arts, the Liguria Study Center, the American Academy in Berlin, the Fine Arts Work Center in Provincetown, and the Radcliffe Institute for Advanced Study. She holds the James A. Michener Chair in Fiction at the University of Texas, Austin, and boy, are her arms tired.

All the Lights
inside My Head Came On

ANNE PERRY
author

MISS MILNE
mathematics

BY THE TIME I WAS ABOUT TWELVE I had missed a lot of school and was behind in mathematics. Since my father was a rather well-known mathematician, better was expected of me. I was at an all-girls school with a headmistress who was small, rotund, and much respected. However, it was the assistant head of whom we were in awe, almost in terror! She was tall and very gaunt. Her one beauty was her hair, which she wore in big "earphones," rather like Princess Leia. Everybody stood obediently for the head, but for the assistant head, Miss Milne, we scattered. She must have thought the school was deserted.

Then doom descended upon my class. We were told that next year Miss Milne would teach us mathematics. We were paralyzed with horror, too numb even to fight — like deer caught in the headlights.

Then the lessons began, geometry, quadratic equations, and so on. Miss Milne was marvelous. All the lights inside my head came on. She was lucid and in her own quiet way, enthusiastic. She passed on not only her understanding of math but her love of it. Suddenly I understood what my father meant when he said that a particular solution to a quadratic equation was more elegant or wittier than another. Sums witty? Are you joking? No. He was right. Even well into my twenties I used to do equations for fun, for pleasure.

There should be a Miss Milne for everyone, for all subjects. History should be an endless, exciting story; geography should be a great exploration; and math should be fun. Thank you to all teachers who turn on the lights!

ANNE PERRY is the internationally bestselling author of more than fifty novels, which have sold over 25 million copies. The *Times* (London) selected her as one of the twentieth century's "100 Masters of Crime." In 2015 she was awarded the Premio de Honor Aragón Negro. Her first series of Victorian crime novels, featuring Thomas and Charlotte Pitt, began with *The Cater Street Hangman*. The latest of these, *The Angel Court Affair*, is her most recent of many appearances on the *New York Times* bestseller list.

In 1990 Perry started a second series of detective novels with the book *The Face of a Stranger*. These are set about thirty-five years before the Pitt series and feature the private detective William Monk and volatile nurse Hester Latterly. The most recent of these (twentieth in the series) is *Corridors of the Night* (April 2015). Perry won an Edgar Award in 2000 with her short story "Heroes." The main character in the story features in an ambitious five-book series set during the First World War. For more, go to www.anneperry.co.uk; www.twitter.com/anneperrywriter; or www.facebook.com/anneperrywriter.

LESLIE EPSTEIN
author

VARIOUS TEACHERS
Los Angeles and Claremont, California

WHAT I REMEMBER is a mélange of teachers, almost all of them associated with a certain fond feeling, but with a few bad apples as well. I know this much: I worked like the devil to get nothing but As for no other conscious reason than the wish not to disappoint these men and women.

Perhaps the fact that my father died when I was young had something to do with it. Yet I was just as industrious before I turned thirteen. All of these folk were in the Los Angeles school system until, a few years after my father's death in 1952, I went to the Webb School in Claremont.

Mrs. (NOT Ms.) Statek, whose name I have surely misspelled, at Canyon Elementary — a place that was then made from World War II Quonset huts. It still is, thanks to Proposition Thirteen. Wild red hair, a dewlap, shaking jowls — and a shaking ruler too. Was she the one who taped my mouth and made me sit in the corner? An excellent lesson, though I remained a wise acre nonetheless.

Mrs. Edwards: short dark hair and a youthful beauty, who

encouraged me to involve myself in the reelection campaign for the fine Mayor Bowren, or Bowron. "Don't be Behind the 'Times'" — then owned by the reactionary branch of the Chandler family — was our excellent shared motto. Brentwood Elementary, perhaps.

Mr. Stegelmayer, Emerson Junior High: shiny-cheeked, four-eyed, with sprouts of hair sticking up in the back, he was an expert and interested history teacher. When I was bitching in my usual fashion about the old fogies who had written the Constitution, he admonished me: "Remember, they were wise enough to construct a means of changing their own document." That quieted me down. And I am sure he was the one (though in a novel about these years I used poetic license to attribute the words to Gregory Peck) who told me, when I was still carrying on about the G.O.P., that the pendulum of history swung left and swung right; when it swung left, however, it always went a little bit further. Those same Republicans do not seem to have learned the laws of physics.

Mr. Edmondson, also at Emerson, or was it freshman year at University High? Tall, rather handsome, I think, and not old: his name and image have stuck in my mind because he was a kind and encouraging figure.

Ah, but Mr. Lindsay, probably at Emerson: yes, he inspired me to try to build a cyclotron (and to hang around the science labs at UCLA, where I was impressed by apples — not Newton's but the ones for sale in automated machines), but he also pinched my ears and was known for doing the same to other lads under his tutelage. Bit suspicious, eh what?

Worst of the lot was Ramsay Harris, who I think was part Malay, and who lived on to be a beloved figure aged one hundred at the Webb School. He played the piano and made up lyrics for our songs and taught God knows what. I never had him in the classroom, but one day I sat at his table for dinner; when the bursary student brought the mystery meat for the night, someone said, "What's THAT?"

"This week's profit," I replied (I told you the duct tape didn't work), and the next morning I was expelled. This same Harris, in one of his year-end poems, wrote, "Les's wit is as sharp as a persimmon / and rumor has it he don't like wimmen." This for distribution to the graduating class and their parents. I wish I were a tunesmith myself: "Old Ramsay pounds the keys to play oldies and blues / But he won't play Gershwin 'cause he don't like Jews." To think I went to the same college as Cole Porter.

But Webb had wonderful instructors: Fred Burr, who coached me in tennis and who had a fit when I only made the wait list at Yale. I never knew what all the fuss was about (I already had my room picked out at Columbia: for some reason I still think I remember it: 141 John Jay Hall) until I actually arrived in New Haven and discovered that not only weren't there many Jews, there weren't any wimmen. Mr. Summner, quite aged, stained by nicotine, smelling of nicotine too, and spitting out tobacco juice as he taught us — and superbly — our lessons in French. *Restez dans la paix, mon vieux.* Jack Iversen, United States history, and a swell guy. And Sam Parkman, not that much older than his students, who strolled down my street in Brookline two years ago and whom I took to a Red Sox game, along with his son, shortly after.

I won't dwell on Yale, except to say that in those days the best part of an education there was the endless lunches in the various colleges — in my case, Trumbull. Alas, the faculty isn't available for those repasts anymore, but in the late fifties Charlie Blitzer and Chet Leib and Jim Hayden would sit with us from noon until we were thrown out at 3:30, day after day, shooting the breeze and teaching us (as all the fine people I have mentioned above taught us) how to put exactly one teaspoon of milk into our cups of coffee — in brief, how to become grown-up citizens in what all too soon would prove to be a difficult world.

P.S. THE WISE ACRE WASN'T DONE: one day, lounging after one of those lunches on York Street, a few of us watched as the famous Richard Lee went into Phil the Barber's, then Fenn-Feinstein, then Barrie's shoes. "What's the mayor doing?" asked one of my straight men. "Four o'clock on Friday," says I, glancing at my watch. "Time to collect." By ten in the morning the next day I was thrown out of Yale too. It was my table mates, I believe, that arranged for me to stay in a house in nearby Hamden (thank you, Jim Hayden, though, sorry, I never learned how to play the recorder), instead of returning, rusticated, to California; and it was Charlie and Chet, in all likelihood, who mounted the campaign (stickers on walls and finally a story in the *New Haven Register*) that caused an abashed dean to call me with the words, "This has not been easy for any of us. Please return.") When I wrote Richard Levin, the Yale president, a few years ago to beg him to reinstate the system that allowed faculty to live and eat in the colleges, he replied, "We are very proud of our college system." That non sequitur caused me to put him in the apple barrel too. Enough. It has been moving to think of these people. Thank you, one, and, in truth, all.

LESLIE EPSTEIN had so many teachers he both loved and hated that he has become a loved and hated teacher himself — for the past thirty years at Boston University's Creative Writing Program. He's also written ten works of fiction and some plays.

[I Have No Idea What They Saw]

DEREK ALGER
author

MR. DUFFY
English, Dwight-Englewood School, Englewood, New Jersey

I'M PROBABLY ABOUT THIRTY YEARS OLDER NOW than Mr. Duffy was when he was my seventh-grade English teacher, and I still can't call him Malcolm. It just doesn't sound right. In my memory, he's Mr. Duffy, strict grammarian and committed devotee of Eugene O'Neill, who taught at the Boys School right after graduating from Dartmouth, and then after it merged with the Girls School, until his recent retirement.

I received an unexpected email from Mr. Duffy the other day, saying he wanted to get together at a local Italian restaurant to tell me about big changes at the school's alumni magazine, with which he has always been very much involved. He signed the email MAD, the *A* standing for his middle name, which I believe was Allan but could have been Aloysius, or Albert, or maybe Andrew, but I'm pretty sure it was Allan, thus giving me the option of writing back "Dear MAD," which I did, thereby avoiding the issue of whether to address him as Malcolm or Mr. Duffy.

A few years ago was the first time I had contact with Mr. Duffy in more than twenty years, and it was all because of a political campaign I ran for the Council of the Borough of Fort Lee, the home on the New Jersey side of the George Washington Bridge, which runs across the Hudson River to Manhattan, or the Bronx, or upstate New York, depending on which lane you choose. I didn't know this at the time, but one of the two council candidates, who was about ten years older than me, was a graduate of the Boys School and very much involved in alumni affairs and events.

That was the initial hook. Armand Pohan, the candidate, mentioned me to Mr. Duffy, who in turn contacted me about an article for the alumni magazine about Armand successfully being elected to the borough council. And then, as it turned out, another of the six council members, whose campaign I had run in the past, was also a graduate of the Boys School; in fact, he was only a year ahead of me, but he didn't stand out because I had no recollection of him being at the same school as me.

The woman who ran the alumni magazine became concerned, and confused, because there didn't seem to be a record of any year in which I graduated. The answer is quite simple; I never graduated from the Boys School. I attended the Boys School for four and a half years, but I had grown my first beard as I was entering my senior year, and the school authorities sent me home the first day, telling me not to come back until I shaved it off.

I was defiant and rebellious, obviously not thinking of the consequences, which led to a huge fight with my father, and the next thing I knew I was living with my aunt, my mother's sister, attending a public high school in Toronto.

I never dreamed I would end up at the hated Englewood

School for Boys, the quintessence in my mind of elitism, old-school WASPs, and those listed in the social register, but the public school system in town was a mess, deteriorating more and more each year as different experiments were applied to create a harmonious integrated utopia of education. Suffice it to say, students of all backgrounds, races, and ethnicities basically imitated their parents, and pandemonium and heightened tension prevailed — not the most optimal environment for learning.

Mr. Duffy and my mother both knew I could write, actually thought I would become a writer long before I had any inkling of it. I have no idea what they saw, or how they knew, but here I am writing this, so they must have known something. I can say this, however: it was only years later that I came to really appreciate what Mr. Duffy had done for me as a teacher.

My first clue that the Board of Education was a bureaucratic nightmare was when my family moved to Englewood, New Jersey, from Queens, New York. My parents bought a house that was five blocks away from Roosevelt Elementary School, which was considered a big plus because my sister and I could walk there. The dividing line between Roosevelt schoolkids and Quarles schoolkids was the street where our new house was. Kids living on our side of the street at the time went to Quarles, while the kids on the south side of the street went to Roosevelt. Apparently, the line was to be moved two blocks north in September, but since we moved in March, the Realtors, or whoever, neglected to tell my parents about this small detail.

As a result, my sister and I were forced to take a bus to Quarles School until the summer, only to become the new kids again that fall when we attended Roosevelt. My parents didn't have the time and resources (and I also had a younger brother and a sister to be cared for) to put up much of a fight, much less prevail against the faceless forces of the Board of Education. Rules are rules, and lines are lines, and what's the big deal, school is school, and they — my sister and I — could take the bus to Quarles for three months or so, and they'd be just fine.

Come fall, my sister and I walked to our new school, Roosevelt, where we began the process of making friends with new classmates all over again. It was at Roosevelt that I began my pattern of performing poorly, or maybe I should say less well than expected, on standardized tests, the so-called Scholastic Aptitude Tests.

The standardized tests were given each year, and based on their results, students were divided into four groups, with one being the highest and four the lowest. Without fail, I always ended up in the second group, but within weeks, I was invariably promoted to the first group, where I usually felt insecure and intimidated, though I never wanted anyone to know.

Fourth grade was the year in which I first learned that the indoctrination we received at school did not necessarily coincide with reality. There were five public elementary schools in Englewood, and it was decided to close one of them, the school where the majority of students were black, and to bus the students there to each of the other four schools.

What I didn't understand at the time was why the kids who were bused from Lincoln School didn't have to show up at school until three days after we did. Our teachers made a point of stressing that the students from Lincoln were no different from us, and that we should greet them warmly, with open arms, and so on. There were already a few black kids at Roosevelt, and I knew many of the Lincoln School guys from Little League, so I never understood what the big deal was. The only lesson I took from the experience was that I was angry the students from Lincoln got an extra three days of summer vacation and I didn't.

The Lincoln bus plan didn't work — in fact, a number of white kids in my class disappeared, never to be seen again — so the next great idea was to create a central sixth-grade school in the old high school building in the middle of town. And that's what they did. When I was in sixth grade, I attended a school completely composed of sixth graders, divided into three teams, with each team occupying a different one of the three floors of the school. How they decided on which team or floor an individual should be assigned to, I have no idea; all I knew was that I was to report to Miss Steinberg in a classroom on the second floor.

Once we all completed sixth grade, which was the only graduation ceremony I ever attended, it was off to the junior high school. By then I was a nervous wreck when it came to almost every class and subject, and the mayhem and overcrowding at the junior high school didn't help. For the first time, I cut school, and as luck, or my ineptitude at breaking rules, would have it, I got snagged. My parents were concerned. I was performing badly in school, but perhaps worse, I was overwhelmed with panic each day while waiting for the bus.

My parents tricked me into taking the entrance exam for the Boys School. I went up to the school, which was high on top of the hill overlooking the rest of Englewood, for an interview with a red-faced, completely bald man who resembled a fiery gnome, and then I was taken to an empty classroom to take a test. My mother encouraged me to take it, said not to worry, that taking the entrance exam by no means meant that I was automatically going to attend the Boys School if I passed.

I've never known of my mother consciously lying to me, so it was probably still open for debate and consideration, or maybe my mother thought I would fail the exam, but that's highly doubtful because she always had much more confidence in me than I ever did. Anyway, I passed the exam, and the next thing I knew, I was hit with major anxiety because I didn't know how to put on a tie and I was an official member of the seventh grade, or the first form, of the Englewood School for Boys.

That's where I first met Mr. Duffy, an oval-faced man with glasses and the demeanor of a scholar, one who loved theater, particularly Shakespeare in the Park, meaning Central Park in New York City, and philharmonic concerts at Lincoln Center. Most of us were scared of Mr. Duffy, but looking back, I think it was more a fear of disappointing him than actual terror, though he did have some unorthodox ways of getting your attention, antics that would probably get him in trouble today since originality and spontaneity are frowned upon.

One of Mr. Duffy's favorite antics, meant to get everyone's attention, would be to interrupt a student who was reciting abysmally incorrect grammar by cracking a yardstick and breaking it over the corner of his desk. Suddenly, the monotone drone of the student was interrupted by a loud whack, and there was Mr. Duffy standing and pointing toward the offender with half a yardstick, the other half lying broken off on the floor.

Now, Mr. Duffy was by no means a tyrant. We knew he wanted what was best for us, to learn about nouns and verbs and such, and dangling participles, and proper clauses, but he did seem like a drill sergeant of the English classroom, though we were never forced to do calisthenics as punishment, instead being compelled to learn additional vocabulary words for any transgressions.

I was annoyed at the time, and I have no idea what prompted him, but Mr. Duffy took special time to tutor me at the end of the school day. Those extra hours really paid off, but of course I didn't see it that way then. My mother certainly did, and she was forever grateful to Mr. Duffy. So, with Mr. Duffy's help, I successfully passed all my final exams, something not heard of at the junior high school, and moved on to eighth grade, not having much to do with Mr. Duffy until eleventh grade, when he was my English teacher once again.

The two things I remember most about eleventh-grade English is that I was introduced to the plays of Eugene O'Neill and also that we were forced to write a composition on different themes every week. As a project for the year, we were given a choice among three writers — Mark Twain, Ernest Hemingway, or Eugene O'Neill — and tasked with reading a biography, as well as the selected writer's major works, and then with writing a term paper on that writer at the end of the spring term.

My grandfather, a prominent educator in Canada, once said, "Study the teacher as well as the subject," which most of my eleventh-grade English class must have intuitively done. Everyone knew Mr. Duffy was the drama director who selected and staged the school's plays, usually two a year, and he also loved Eugene O'Neill, so for our project, fourteen of us selected O'Neill and one very stuck-up and unpopular kid chose Mark Twain, which by no means is a reflection on Twain.

Another memory that stands out quite vividly is of us all sitting in a semicircle in chairs with a small mini-desk on the right arm — lefties were in trouble — waiting for Mr. Duffy. I was sitting next to the window, with a kid named Hiller next to me, and Hiller was telling a story and ended up loudly saying "Fuck" just as Mr. Duffy entered the room. The entire class froze in silence as we all waited and wondered what Mr. Duffy's reaction would be, most thinking Hiller was doomed.

Mr. Duffy stood straight-faced in front of his desk, allowing the tension to build, letting us all dwell in the eternity of the moment, waiting for what we thought would be a tremendous explosion. Then finally, after a few minutes, Mr. Duffy spoke.

"Mr. Hiller, I am not impressed," he said. Here it comes, we thought. "The word *fuck* has been so overused that it has ceased to have any shock value. Let me give you a sentence. 'Fucking fuckers fuck.'" Mr. Duffy paused. "There you have the word *fuck* used as a noun, a verb, and an adjective, and I defy you, Mr. Hiller, to tell me what that sentence means."

No answer was forthcoming. Hiller wisely didn't say anything, and class continued as usual.

I first realized how valuable Mr. Duffy had been as an English teacher during my freshman year of college. You could tell I was a freshman because I took a course at 8:30 AM on Tuesdays and Thursdays, a course on Shakespeare's history plays. The first play we read was *Richard II*, and I remember that on the second Tuesday of the course, the teacher asked us to write a four-page paper on Bolingbroke's motives for overthrowing and deposing Richard before the next class. I found the paper easy to write, and though most would never know this, nor would I have admitted it, I actually enjoyed writing it.

Late the night before the next class, I was amazed and astounded to discover many members of the class freaking out, their papers still not done, most of them having tremendous difficulty writing such a paper. I didn't understand. Everyone in the class was highly intelligent, a number were self-proclaimed intellectuals, and yet, despite most of them being far more aware of culture than I was, at least in terms of art and music, and all of them world travelers, while I had never crossed the

Mississippi River at the time, much less an ocean, they couldn't write.

That's when it hit me. Mr. Duffy, of course. High school English, weekly compositions, writing those goddamned compositions, had prepared me for college far more than I ever expected. So, as I grew older, just as I began to see and appreciate more and more the influence my mother had been, I also saw that I owed a major debt of gratitude to Mr. Duffy, which I hope to let him know when we finally meet at the local Italian restaurant.

DEREK ALGER was a graduate of the MFA fiction writing program at Columbia University, a contributing editor at *Serving House Journal*, and a former editor at large at *Pif* magazine, where more than a hundred of his interviews with writers have been published over a period of fourteen years. Alger's fiction and essays appear in *Confrontation*, *Del Sol Review*, *Ducts.org*, the *Literary Review*, and *Writers Notes*, among others.

[He Was So Passionate about Reading]

CJ LYONS
author

MR. TOBIN
English

I'VE BEEN A STORYTELLER ALL MY LIFE — something that led to many hours placed in time-outs, since my parents and teachers decided I had difficulty telling the difference between fact and fiction, aka truth and lies.

Of course, all that time spent in time-out meant more time spent listening to the voices in my head, which led to writing those stories down as soon as I was old enough. But I never told anyone about my notebooks filled with fanciful characters and their adventures. I kept them private; they were my way of making sense of the world around me.

Until seventh-grade English class and a teacher named Mr. Tobin. He was one of those teachers who was so passionate about reading and the power of stories to change the world that few kids who walked through his classroom doors emerged unchanged.

Mr. Tobin created literary scavenger hunts through time, geography, and genre that would have you reading Edgar Rice

Burroughs's *John Carter of Mars* one week and *The Last of the Mohicans* the next. He encouraged debate, often tying the origins of current events to literary and pop-culture influences.

Most of all, he made us write. We didn't have to share our work with the world — he understood that shining a spotlight on our innermost feelings would be the worst humiliation possible for a seventh grader — but thanks to him, we learned the power that words hold.

Thanks to Mr. Tobin, I won my first award for writing and had my first short story published. I wonder if he has any clue what he started by giving me the courage to share my words with the world.

CJ Lyons, the *New York Times*– and *USA Today*–bestselling author of twenty-nine novels and a former pediatric ER doctor, has lived the life she writes about in her cutting-edge Thrillers with Heart. Her novels have won the International Thriller Writers' prestigious Thriller Award, the RT Reviewers' Choice Award, the Readers' Choice Award, the RT Seal of Excellence, and the Daphne du Maurier Award for Excellence in Mystery and Suspense. Learn more about Lyons's Thrillers with Heart at www.cjlyons.net.

[Renowned for Her High Standards]

THOMAS KANE
economist

MS. GILROY, GERTRUDE SHERMAN, SISTER REGINA BELL,
MR. HICKS, SISTER RITA XAVIER, DAVID ELLWOOD
St. Leo Catholic School, Winston-Salem, North Carolina, and
Bishop McGuinness High School, Winston-Salem, North Carolina

IN FOURTH GRADE my teacher was Ms. Gilroy. I was a shy, reserved student. I got along with my classmates well, but I kept a low profile. When the class was asked to perform *A Christmas Carol* in front of the school community (parents and students), Ms. Gilroy asked me to play the lead. I recall memorizing my lines, practicing with my fellow students in her basement. In fact, I still remember my opening line, "Cratchett, get back to work!" Her confidence in me is what launched me.

In fifth and sixth grade, my teacher was Gertrude Sherman — a teacher renowned in my school for her high standards. Her nickname was the "Sherman Tank." She asked us to diagram sentences every day, on the board in front of the room. She was not warm like Ms. Gilroy, but she had high expectations for us. She gave me a bookmark at the end of the year with the words "Marching to the beat of a different drummer." That made me feel special — a feeling that has lasted to this day. There is no question that I'm a better writer today because of Mrs. Sherman.

In eighth grade, Sister Regina Bell taught me math. Until that point, I had done well in math but did not realize I had not been challenged. As a result, I took math for granted — I was not inspired by its beauty. By the end of the year, I not only believed math was beautiful but wanted to learn more.

In tenth grade, Mr. Vonnie Hicks taught me biology. I learned a tremendous amount from Mr. Hicks — about science, as well as about being an active citizen, about social justice. He supervised us as we built sets for the school play. My commitment to public service began with Mr. Hicks. I also learned now to operate a jigsaw, which I remember every time I pick up the tool in my basement.

In eleventh and twelfth grade, Sr. Rita Xavier taught me chemistry and physics. Sr. Rita had worked with Dr. Wernher von Braun yet gave that up to join the convent and become a teacher. She was a brilliant woman who had high standards as well as a twinkle in her eye. I worked hard to live up to her standards, and I feel like I'm still doing that today.

In graduate school, my mentor was David Ellwood. I was always amazed that in a research seminar, David was the first to recognize the central flaw or insight in any paper. He also had faith in me, and I'm sure I never would have pushed to the next level without that faith.

I'm now thinking about others — Christopher Jencks, Jennifer Warlick, Richard Zeckhauser — who had similar impacts. Perhaps that's why I'm now devoting myself to helping schools develop the systems required to recognize their most effective teachers — using student surveys and classroom observations, as well as student achievement gains.

THOMAS J. KANE is an economist and Walter H. Gale Professor of Education at the Harvard Graduate School of Education. He is faculty director of the Center for Education Policy Research, a university-wide research center that works with school districts and state agencies.

[He Thought I Was Smart]

ALAN DERSHOWITZ
lawyer

MR. KEIN
eighth grade, Yeshiva Etz Chaim, Brooklyn, New York

I WAS A TERRIBLE STUDENT through the first seven grades of elementary school. Even my parents lost faith in me, as evidenced by the following story. My elementary school had a three-track system. I was on the lowest track. When the school administered an IQ test and I got the highest score in the school, they moved me from the third track to the first. My mother ran to school complaining that the test must have been a mistake and that I could never compete with the smart kids in the first track. So they compromised and put me in the middle track, where I continued to get Cs in the academic subjects and Ds in conduct and discipline.

Everything changed in the eighth grade when my teacher, Mr. Kein, called me in for a talk. He told me something nobody had ever told me before. He said I was smart. At first I thought he meant that I was a "smart aleck," which others had already told me, or a "wise guy," which was my reputation. But he really meant it. He insisted that my grades didn't reflect my intelligence and that I was underperforming. He recognized that I was restless and easily bored. Today I would probably be diagnosed with attention deficit disorder. To my Yiddish-speaking teachers I simply did not have *zitsfleish*, which literally means enough fat on my butt to allow me to sit for long periods. Whatever the reason, I was constantly squirming in class, looking at the clock, and daydreaming about playing punchball, rooting for the Brooklyn Dodgers, flirting with the girls, or telling jokes.

Mr. Kein was the first teacher to recognize my potential. He treated me as an intelligent student capable of dealing with the most complex issues, while recognizing that I was not highly motivated. He understood that it was his role to motivate me, and he did so by playing to my strengths. It worked — I did much better in the eighth grade than I had done earlier.

Then I went to high school, where my teachers continued to treat me as a failure. I did poorly in high school, except on competitive statewide examinations. When I won a New York state scholarship, despite my low grades, my principal suspected me of cheating, until he checked to see who was sitting around me on the state scholarship exam and discovered that there were no good students in the area from whom I could copy.

I made it to Brooklyn College by the skin of my teeth. Fortunately, they had an admission process that combined high school grades with test scores on a competitive exam, and I did well on the exam. When I got into college, Mr. Kein called me and reminded me of my worth. I did well in college, and I am certain that I owe much of my academic success to the first teacher who told me I was smart.

ALAN DERSHOWITZ is a lawyer, jurist, and political commentator. At the age of twenty-eight he became the youngest full professor at Harvard Law School.

[We Knew What Love Was]

ALEX SHOUMATOFF
author

STAN FERET, math, ROSEMARIE DONAHUE, English,
PAUL FISHER, geography,
Bedford Rippowam School, Bedford, New York

I GREW UP IN BEDFORD, NEW YORK, a privileged exurb in
northern Westchester County, forty miles north of New York
City. From the fourth to the eighth grade I attended the local
private school, Bedford Rippowam. The teachers were excep-
tional, particularly Stan Feret, who taught me so much math
that I completed all my math requirements for the rest of my
life by the time I was thirteen. He taught me how to analyze
a problem and craft a solution to it by proceeding from one
logical step to the next — an invaluable skill in any endeavor.
Rosemarie Donahue, my English teacher, had us graphing
complicated sentences with multiple subordinate clauses,
participial phrases, and adverbs modifying adjectives. She
awakened in me a lifelong fascination with the construction
of sentences, the flow and order of their clauses, the sound of
their words.

Paul Fisher, who taught geography, had us writing re-
ports on far-off cultures. I did one on Liberia and another on

Tibet and got an A-plus on both. Little did I know, but this would become my profession. These teachers imparted to us impressive quantities of information, but even more important, although we may not have been fully conscious of it at the time, they taught us about love. We had been nurtured and mentally turned on in an atmosphere of love. Never again would so much attention and reinforcement be lavished on us. Never again would life be so fair. Never again would we be so well rewarded for coming up with the right answer, and never again would the right answer be so clear.

ALEX SHOUMATOFF revisits his wonderful boyhood with great teachers like Stan Feret in his eleventh book, *From Bedford to Borneo: The Education of an Animist* (2016). He's written more than a hundred long magazine pieces for *Vanity Fair*, the *New Yorker*, and other publications, and he is the editor of DispatchesFromTheVanishingWorld.com, which he launched in 2001 to raise consciousness about the planet's fast-disappearing biocultural diversity.

PART THREE

High School

[With Love and High Hopes]

MARIANA KLAVENO

actor

BRUCE HOLBERT, English,
LOUISE BRAUN, American literature and French,
St. John High School, St. John, Washington

I GREW UP IN AN AREA most people would consider the middle of nowhere. A wheat farmer's daughter, I was born and raised in an extremely rural farming community in the eastern part of Washington State. I now live in Los Angeles, which feels about as far from the wheat fields as you can get. It's a city in which fortunes are spent on preschool, and private high schools serve as status symbols for the parents. Since being asked to write this, I've reflected quite a bit on the education I received back home. It's humble by comparison to the kind of schooling people receive here in LA, but I can't help feeling a sense of pride about it nonetheless. There wasn't any choice involved; everyone simply attended the local public school. Yet I feel fortunate to say I've been inspired by several wonderful teachers along the way. I'm going to break the rule and talk about two teachers instead of just one, and I had them both in high school.

What is so particularly torturous about high school? John

Hughes addressed that query in his films far better than I ever could in a few pages. What I do know is that it's a time when everything you once knew is suddenly thrown into question. It's confusing, frustrating, often humiliating, and full of angst. My experience of high school was no different, even though by most standards I had an easy time of it. I wasn't bullied. I had a lot of friends and a supportive family, and I was involved in sports and a number of other activities. Despite these advantages, I still considered those four years as something to suffer through, something to survive. I owe my survival in large part to Mrs. Braun and Mr. Holbert.

Louise Braun was my American literature and French teacher. She'd been teaching for decades before I reached high school, so I'd heard many stories about her before I even stepped foot in her classroom. Mrs. Braun was eccentric. She wore a wig some days for no discernible reason other than the desire to have hair that was short and curly instead of long and straight. She smoked unapologetically. She took a group of us on a trip to New York that wasn't sponsored by the school. She did it independently because she thought it was important that we be exposed to all that the big city has to offer, most notably the museums and the theater. She had a razor-sharp perception, a soft voice, and a brilliant intellect. I found her utterly fascinating.

Bruce Holbert was my English teacher. Because he'd also taught my three older siblings, as with Mrs. Braun, his reputation preceded him. Mr. Holbert was known for being tough. Not mean — tough. He ruined many a straight-A streak, including mine, and I must admit that knowing he'll read this strikes a long-forgotten fear in my heart. I half expect to receive a copy in the mail with his dreaded red pen pointing out every weak transition and grammatical error. He demanded a great deal of us, which made me want that A even more. What I appreciate the most was the sophistication of the material and projects he assigned. We studied and wrote about the works of Joseph Campbell and Herman Hesse in a way that was anything but conventional. Nothing was dumbed down. He trusted that we could rise to the occasion. It's remarkable how hard you'll work for someone who believes in you rather than patronizes you. I've had more than a few teachers over the years who coasted along on autopilot mode. Mr. Holbert doesn't have an autopilot mode.

Despite their differences, Mrs. Braun and Mr. Holbert shared a characteristic whose value cannot be overstated. They treated us all like adults. They did so even when we had no business being treated as such. I cringe when I think how obnoxious I must have been, listening to Nirvana, reading *The Catcher in the Rye*, and daring to believe I had an original thought in my head. Yet both teachers engaged me with an openness lacking in any judgment. They did this not only with me but with every student. It didn't matter if you were a jock, a cowboy, a nerd, a teacher's pet, or an outcast. Mrs. Braun was just as comfortable talking to the cheerleaders as she was to the troublemaking "bad boys." In heated philosophical debates, Mr. Holbert gave the same valued platform to the students who were more comfortable in metal shop as he did to those of us who fancied ourselves intellectuals. Their investment in all of us was genuine and deeply personal. I doubt they realized how well they were working in tandem. Mr. Holbert pushed our minds and abilities beyond our comfort zones, and if we fell short, Mrs. Braun was there with an immeasurable kernel of wisdom or a reassuring anecdote about the human condition. Their influence extended beyond the classroom curriculum. At a time when we were all struggling in various ways, they were there to place an appropriate book in our hands or to simply lend a sympathetic ear. They let us know that we were respected and that we weren't alone. I marvel at the compassion needed to take on class after class of angst-ridden teenagers, and I wonder if there wasn't something of a tortured artist inside both Mrs. Braun and Mr. Holbert. How else could they guide us along that particularly rocky road so well?

After graduation they each sat me down separately, urging me to study and pursue my quiet dream of acting. Considering where I grew up, this was quite a revolutionary idea. It terrified as much as it excited me. I remember quite well my conversation with Mr. Holbert, and the strength of his encouragement helped to steel my resolve. His faith in me left an indelible mark on me. For that, and for all those red marks, I thank you, Mr. Holbert.

I stayed in touch with Mrs. Braun after graduation through letters and lunches when I was back home, as did many of her former students. She continued to be an influence and a friend. Mrs. Braun passed away several years ago, before I became a working actor in film and television. As a graduation present she gave me a copy of *Walden*, her favorite book, and I still keep it with me. In it she inscribed, "With love and high hopes."

I sincerely hope I haven't let her down.

MARIANA KLAVENO was born and raised in the rural farming area of the Palouse in Eastern Washington State. After studying drama at the University of Washington in Seattle, she moved to Los Angeles to pursue her acting career in television and film. She has appeared in *ER*, *Dexter*, *True Blood*, *Devious Maids*, *West of Redemption*, and *Stalker*. She continues to reside in Los Angeles with her husband.

[Full of Thinking and Caring]

GEORGE SAUNDERS
author

MR. LINDBLOOM, geology,
MS. WILLIAMS, English,
Oak Forest High School, Oak Forest, Illinois

WHEN I WAS A SENIOR IN HIGH SCHOOL, my career plan was: There was this kid in our school who knew someone who knew someone who knew this guy who knew someone in the Eagles. This kid was putting together a sort of all-star band that would, through the special intervention of the guy who knew the guy who knew the guy, be opening, next fall, for the band that opened for the band that sometimes opened for the Eagles. My initial incredulity was disabled a bit when I went with this kid to a local music store, and he pulled out a check, to the store, from United Artists, in the sum of $10,000, to buy a new P.A. I still don't understand what the heck was actually going on there. But, flash-forwarding: the band never played a single gig.

I was, in other words, on the path to nowhere — but would have only found this out a year or two later.

Luckily I was in the sphere of influence of two wonderful teachers.

In Ms. Williams's English classes, she sometimes showed filmstrips on the topic of "great American authors." Here was Melville, gesturing at a whale, who was obligingly surfacing. Here was Nathanial Hawthorne, looking pensive under a cherry tree. Ms. Williams seemed to love these writers. Like every other kid in our school with any taste, I had a big crush on Ms. Williams. She was beautiful, luminous; her intelligence fierce, her sense of humor dry. What did she love about these American authors, anyway? I sat entranced, wondering. Their minds, it seemed, their boldness, the lives they'd led, full of thinking and caring, devoid of indifference, habit, servility. I longed to be worthy of her attention, someone who might appear in a filmstrip himself someday. Perhaps that filmstrip would show me sitting right here, in my little fold-down desk, at Oak Forest High School, praying for Ms. Williams to glance my way and approve.

Ms. Williams was actually dating my geology teacher, Mr. Lindbloom. They made a kind of intellectual power couple. Every Friday he gave his class over to free discussion. Why are we here? Why does evil so often win? How should we live? Those things that you know: how do you know them? Are you sure about them? During one of the Friday sessions, I raised my hand and said…something. I don't remember what it was. Given my reading at the time (Kahlil Gibran and liner notes for art-rock bands), it was probably something along the lines of: "Suffer the children to learn that love shall leaven the bread by which, children of the stars, ye shall thrive, if only you do not, like sages of yore, wrest your eyes in futile languor." Whatever it was, Mr. Lindbloom saw something in it, and after class, asked me to write it down. It was always better if you wrote it down, he said. It was good discipline. It clarified the thought.

That night, as I sat in front of a clean sheet of paper, I imagined — well, I imagined Mr. Lindbloom and Ms. Williams and a few of the other young teachers, gathered at a bar in... not a bar, no. That was common. A mansion. A secret mansion one of them owned, reserved for intellectual discussion.

Mr. Lindbloom takes out my paper.

"Here's something interesting," he says to his friends. "I won't tell you who wrote it. But see if you can guess."

Then he reads: "Even as the stars are aloft, so too may we, rending unto Zeus, saying nay to Mordor, rise above the blackened plain of the Timid, exalting the stars, even unto the generation."

A respectful silence.

"Shakespeare?" someone says.

"Kahlil Gibran?" someone else says.

"Lincoln?"

"Actually," Mr. Lindbloom says, "this was written by one of my students."

"Must be someone pretty special," Ms. Williams says.

"Saunders," Mr. Lindbloom says.

"You've got to be kidding!" says one of the lesser members of the group, who will soon get kicked out for being so mundane.

"I had a feeling," Ms. Williams says. "There's definitely something going on there."

A more honest part of me knew very well where this was headed and was thinking: I'm going to all this trouble and he'll never even mention it again. He probably already forgot he asked for it. And then I'll have to stop loving him. That's sort of how it was in our school. Teachers were busy. Most of them seemed a little heartbroken to me, as if the time when they'd actually expected a kid to benefit from their attention was long past.

I wrote it out anyway.

I handed it over on Friday. Mr. Lindbloom pulled me aside on Monday. To thank me. That afternoon Ms. Williams told me that she read it, too, and thought it was good, really interesting, I should keep it up, keep writing things down as they came to me.

Together, they conspired to get me a copy of *Atlas Shrugged*, and I took it home over Christmas break. I read all 1,084 pages of it, on a car trip, and when I finished the novel, there in the back seat of Andy Fiedler's Nova, I had a sudden image of myself, wearing what I thought of as "a college sweater," pacing feverishly across a tree-dense campus, strenuously explaining my philosophical viewpoint to a group of braless co-eds much taken with philosophers and philosophy, and then we all headed over to the football game, holding those little shouting-cone deals.

When I got home, I called the guy who knew the guy who knew the guy, quit the band and started trying to get into college.

But there was a problem: I had flunked two classes and had literally never studied outside of school, except once, when I made a cassette of the answers to a biology quiz and went to sleep with the tape on, hoping to learn by aural osmosis. I was rejected by Notre Dame (fair enough) and the Berklee College of Music (ditto, didn't actually read music) but got into a state school where the main requirement seemed to be ownership of a bong. Mr. Lindbloom felt I deserved better. He made a call, to the Colorado School of Mines. As a grad student in geology, he'd met a number of heavy-hitters in the field who had gone there. Somehow, in a single 10-minute call, he persuaded them to give me a try.

How did he do it? Why did he do it? Would I have done it? Would I go to such lengths for one of my students, now that I'm a teacher myself? Good Lord, I hope so. But I don't know. Time moves fast, and, in teaching, at a real-life pace, you never really know who needs what.

All I had to do, the School of Mines said, was pass 18 summer-school hours of remedial math and science.

Which, appalled at the thought of letting Mr. Lindbloom/ Ms. Williams down, I did.

And that fall I went off to college.

Now, at this distance, I can see how important and unlikely these teacherly interventions were. They were young teachers (in their mid-20s), they were making lives for themselves, they were surrounded every day by hundreds of us blustering, cynical, musk-smelling 1970s kids, resisting positive influence with all our sneering Aerosmith-inflected might. It all could have been different for me and would have been, if not for whatever it is that makes an older person — busy person, tired person, finite person — turn toward a young person and say, in whatever way is needed: "Of course you can. Why not? Give it a try."

SLIGHT P.S.: Mr. Lindbloom and Ms. Williams married a few years later, taught in that same school another 30 years, and only recently retired. I do the math of that sometimes: how many kids, over the course of those years, got the benefit of their loving attention? How many people are incrementally more thoughtful, curious, and open — how many people think slightly better of themselves and their abilities, are more capable of change, love, generosity, rebound — because of these two examples of that precious race, the true teacher?

It must run into the hundreds, even thousands, if you count (as you must) the children of those children directly influenced. As one of those thus benefited, I retain the mute, head-shaking gratitude of someone snatched back from the edge of an abyss.

I would have lived, sure, but not nearly as well.

GEORGE SAUNDERS is an American writer of short stories, essays, novellas, and children's books. His writing has appeared in the *New Yorker*, *Harper's*, *McSweenys*, and *GQ*. He also contributed a weekly column, "American Psyche," to the weekend magazine of the *Guardian* until October 2008. A professor at Syracuse University, Saunders won the National Magazine Award for fiction four times and the second prize in the O. Henry Awards in 1997. His first story collection, *CivilWarLand in Bad Decline*, was a finalist for the 1996 PEN/Hemingway Award. In 2006 Saunders received a MacArthur Fellowship and the World Fantasy Award for his short story "CommComm."

RAISED AS A MILITARY BRAT, I attended eleven different schools during my first twelve years of school. I never made many lasting friendships, and I struggled in school, even if I typically scored high on standardized tests.

Most of my teachers considered me a slacker, one of life's perennial losers. And they had little patience either for my sloppy schoolwork or my occasional attempts to ward off the droning boredom of class by acting out.

But I can remember a few exceptions. Miss Willis in fourth grade, for one, whose unfailing patience at my failure to turn in homework was a kindness I'll never be able to repay. Or the soft-hearted substitute teacher I had in seventh grade whose plaintive "Good-bye, Dan" washed over me as I rushed to catch the afternoon bus on the final day of school.

The one I remember most, though, was Bonnie Voss, my senior-year English teacher.

We didn't start off well. My best friend, Ed, and I were in

the same class, and we were a disruptive duo. Ed was transferred out after the first week, and I spent the next few weeks sitting at a desk near the front of the room so that no-nonsense Miss Voss could keep me in check.

Yet as the first semester went on, I began to find the work interesting. I remember having to memorize the "Tomorrow and tomorrow and tomorrow" soliloquy from *Macbeth* and, perhaps for the first time, actually understanding what Shakespeare was trying to say. Slowly, my grade — at least in English — improved.

The real change occurred near the end of the semester, when Miss Voss approached me with an invitation. She would be forming an elective course for the second semester — my final semester of high school — that would focus on world literature. She was approaching some of the smartest students in school.

And she wanted to know if I was interested in attending too.

Amazed, a little intimidated, and yet strangely pleased, I said yes. And that simple act performed by a demanding teacher made all the difference. Over the next few months, I read Camus's *The Stranger*, Dostoevsky's *Crime and Punishment*, and Orwell's *1984*, among other great works. And I loved every one of them.

I was far from the best student in class. That would have been difficult. One of my classmates was bound on a full scholarship to the prestigious College of William & Mary. But I held my own. And I received one of the highest grades of my high school career.

I can't even say it made an immediate difference. I barely graduated from high school, and I ended up flunking out of two different colleges, which led to my joining the army in

1967. College professors, I discovered, were less willing even than high school teachers to indulge indifferent students.

But three years later, when I left the army, I was ready. I returned to college and began working hard. I made the dean's list my first semester in junior college, and I ended up graduating with honors from the University of California, San Diego. My major: English and American literature.

I even went on to earn a master's degree in journalism at the University of Oregon, after which I embarked on a three-decade-plus career as a journalist.

Shakespeare wrote, "We know what we are, but know not what we may be." A good teacher can, sometimes, recognize the potential that sits silent within us. While I was the one who did the work, I recognize the debt I owe to Miss Voss. Without her patience, her firm guidance, and her faith in my abilities, I might never have straightened out.

I will be forever in her debt.

DAN WEBSTER is a career journalist who has written for newspapers, magazines, radio, and online news organizations. He was a film reviewer for the *Spokesman-Review* from 1984 to 2009 and has reviewed films for Spokane Public Radio since 1999.

[Never without His Hat]

Marya Hornbacher
author

Jack Driscoll
creative writing, Interlochen Center for the Arts, Interlochen, Michigan

I DON'T THINK I'VE EVER SEEN Driscoll without his hat. I'm sure he has a regular head under there, just like he must have a face beneath his beard; but I've never seen either, and likely never will. The man is attached to his hat. It's part of his character. He's a character in the story of my time at boarding school, where all the teachers had only last names — the others were Delp, Bozanic, Caszatt. Driscoll may be known as Jack to his friends, but that's of no concern to me. To me, he's Driscoll, baseball capped, gray bearded, and forever wearing jeans.

Jack Driscoll is a phenomenal novelist and poet, which I knew when I was shuffling into an 8:00 AM workshop, half asleep in my blue uniform (okay, it may have been pajamas — the only rule was "wear blue"), but didn't fully grasp till I was older. That figures; Driscoll had the poor luck to have me in his workshop when I was fifteen and sixteen, and I was perhaps overmuch enamored of Plath at the time. But it was on Driscoll's wry, gruff watch that I actually learned to write, such as I can. No, he didn't teach me to write — he taught me to *see*. What I remember of Plath are the red tulips, the exact red that he made me suddenly see clear as day when he read the poem aloud. It was in his workshop that I realized that I was in love not only with words but with images — the precise shimmer of the lake as a northern pike flipped and twisted out of it, the curve of the prow of a fishing boat cutting through the water at dawn. He's a midwestern writer and made me realize I was one as well, and that the hard land, broad prairie, and thick woods where I'm from were subject enough to occupy me for a lifetime. The visible, tactile world had always consumed me, but I hadn't yet learned to put it into words; it was Driscoll who taught me to paint with my pen.

I remember the first time I truly understood how to write a poem: I was scowling at a piece of paper, trying to invent something pompous and inflated — what the hell do you write about when you're fifteen, sixteen? — and I suddenly in one mad dash wrote a poem called "In the Bra Department of Dayton's." I stared at it, horrified. What good was a poem about buying your first *bra*? Who cares? What does it matter, in some cosmic sense? It doesn't, of course. But it was *true*. Driscoll was always going on about the *emotional truth* of writing: he wanted your writing to be from the gut, real, honest, something that cut to the core. And this poem did. I could *feel* that it did. I handed it in and wandered out the door in a haze. I floated for days on the high from writing one true poem — it was a feeling I wanted to have again, and again, and again. When I got the poem back from Driscoll, it was almost invisible in the scramble of red pen — but at the end, there were his words, in the inimitable Driscoll block-lettered hand: GOOD POEM.

If I had an in-house Driscoll now, I'd throw this blasted book I'm trying to write at his head and blame him for the whole endeavor. The best I can do is shoot him an email, congratulate him on his retirement and on all the writers he's turned out over the years, tell him I miss him, and blame this whole endeavor on his hat.

MARYA HORNBACHER is the author of five books, including *Madness: A Bipolar Life* and the 1998 Pulitzer Prize nominee for nonfiction *Wasted: A Memoir of Anorexia and Bulimia*.

Shaped and Furiously Polished by My Teachers

DAVID BELLOS
translator and biographer

MR. BROGDEN, Latin, MR. PRYCE, German,
MR. ALLSOP, geography, MR. SMITH, French,
Westcliff High School, Essex, United Kingdom

THE DEDICATION OF MY LAST BOOK, which is about translation, is *In Memory of My Teachers*. I guess that's why I have been asked to contribute to this volume. I am very happy to do so and to expand my dedication into a brief memoir of my school days.

I was educated in the 1950s, in a small town in the south of England. I gained entry to a state-funded but academically selective grammar school for boys (like most educational institutions of the time, it was a single-sex school but fortunately located next door to the girls' school). Westcliff High was keen on excellence — keen to prove it was as good as any Eton or Harrow, and keen to get its boys way out ahead and if possible into university, at a time when only about 4 percent of the age group pursued postsecondary education. I suffered horribly from that sense of *needing to excel*. But I profited from it more than I could possibly realize at the time.

Around the age of twelve or thirteen, I realized, or perhaps just decided (as one does at that age), that I was no good at math, geography, music, or art, and pretty hopeless at all forms of sport, being a short and weedy sort of lad. What was left? Languages! Languages were being promoted heavily at that time: the next generation, our teachers said, just had to get to know our European neighbors better — our old and present enemies included. As a result, a raft of languages was offered, and I took them all: Latin, of course, and French, like almost everyone, and also German, and then Russian too. I was so well taught that I ended up a professor of languages at Princeton, some thirty-five years later. In the interval, I must have learned a few things here and there, but the bedrock of what I know now, of what I teach, and what I write about, was laid down, shaped, and furiously polished by my teachers at Westcliff High School for Boys between 1956 and 1962.

Mr. Brogden was my Latin teacher. He was a color-blind eccentric, and on various occasions in the summer he turned up for school in his pajama bottoms, since he couldn't tell them from cotton slacks. Alas, he didn't think much of me, and he was right: Latin never was my thing. When I set off for Cambridge to take an entrance exam (which I failed, of course) he wished me bon voyage in the following words, spoken in his ominous basso profundo: "Enjoy your trip to Cambridge, Bellos. It will be your last."

Mr. Pryce taught me German. He was a jittery man who never stopped smiling as he hemmed and hawed, trying to find the right words in English — but he was a completely different man when speaking German. Drops of sweat would trickle down his neck, mysteriously rising somewhere on the shiny surface of his large and entirely bald pate. I think he was a bit scared of me; I think he was a bit scared in general. But he showed me that if you learn to speak another language well, you can be someone else for a time. It's something that has helped me enormously throughout my life.

Mr. Allsop was a geography teacher who had learned Russian during his military service (thousands of young Britons were put through intensive Russian at the Joint Services School of Languages in the early years of the Cold War). He agreed to teach me and a handful of other boys that beautiful and difficult language after school hours, three times a week, using a tiny room that was, I believe, intended as a storeroom or closet. He was passionate, patient, and infinitely encouraging. I don't suppose he got any pay or credit for those extra hours he put in. He left me with an indelible memory of a few poems by Pushkin and a confusion about conditional sentences in Russian that no number of subsequent teachers and grammar books has ever managed to put right.

The man who has and surely deserves the softest spot in my heart, however, was Mr. Smith, who taught French. A small, slight man with a mop of silvery hair, he had (or so we believed) "done something important" during the war, and his spoken French, despite the slight lisp that he had in both his languages, was (I now realize) flawless. He imparted his accent to me and some other boys in a matter of weeks. As a result I don't think I've ever not had a native accent in French since the age of eleven.

Despite his mild, easygoing manner, Mr. Smith had no difficulty at all keeping order in a roomful of thirty-five teenage boys. Quietly, smilingly, he just imposed himself. He knew what he was about. Nobody tried to rag him, not even the tearaways who regularly pitted their wits and their anger against other masters.

From Mr. Smith I learned French grammar from top to bottom, alongside bits of La Fontaine and Voltaire, Giraudoux and Anouilh. He set me up! I've done nothing but exploit, build on, and apply the things he taught me throughout what is now my own very long career.

The best lessons he taught me were of a slightly different order. *Know your subject and then people will listen; love your subject and then people will follow.*

Because I knew that from experience at school, I've never bothered too much about pedagogical theory, teacher training, or educational protocols. Not that they aren't perfectly proper and sometimes necessary, but the bottom line for a teacher of anything to anybody is just that: *Know your subject, love your subject.* The rest will come on its own.

When I was at school my teachers appeared immensely old to me. For a long time I assumed that Mr. Brogden, Mr. Pryce, Mr. Allsop, and Mr. Smith were long dead. I now realize that they may not have been more than a decade or two older than me. So it's possible, even plausible, that one or more of them is still alive. I do hope so. I would like them to know that though I may not have been a particularly memorable student or particularly interesting to teach, I remain, after half a century, nothing more than the product of their work.

DAVID BELLOS was educated at Westcliff High in Essex and at Oxford University, where he studied modern languages. After teaching in several British universities, he came to the United States in 1997 and is now a professor of French and comparative literature at Princeton, where he also directs the Program in Translation and Intercultural Communication. Bellos has written biographies of Georges Perec (1993) and Jacques Tati (1999), which have been translated into many languages, and an introduction to translation studies, *Is That a Fish in Your Ear?: The Amazing Adventure of Translation* (2011). He has translated numerous authors from French and offers a new understanding of the life and work of Romain Gary in *Romain Gary: A Tall Story* (2010). He is currently writing a book about *Les Misérables*.

[The Writer inside Me]

TESS GERRITSEN
author

MISS HUTCHINSON
English, Stephen Watts Kearny High School, San Diego, California

AS AN ASIAN AMERICAN GIRL growing up in California, I faced powerful family and cultural pressure to pursue a "practical" career, so at the urging of my parents, I ended up going to medical school. Yet what I really wanted to be, from a very young age, was a writer. And Miss Viletta Hutchinson, my tenth-grade English teacher, recognized the writer inside me. She nurtured me, she cornered my parents to praise my talent, and sometimes she pushed me up in front of the class to share my work. For years after I graduated, we continued to correspond. I left medicine and eventually did become a novelist. Every year, Miss Hutchinson would write to tell me that she liked my latest book. Every year I could expect her annual Christmas card, addressed to me in her spidery hand, detailing her latest adventures in retirement, the countries she'd visited, the plays she'd attended. Then one year, no Christmas card came, even though I had faithfully sent her one, as I always did. A few months later, I received a kind note from her

cousin, telling me that Miss Hutchinson had passed away —
and that she had never stopped talking about me, the student
she'd always known would be a writer.

Tess Gerritsen, internationally bestselling author, took an unusual
route to her writing career. A graduate of Stanford University, she went
on to medical school at the University of California, San Francisco,
where she was awarded her MD. While on maternity leave from her
work as a physician, she began to write fiction. In 1987 her first novel
was published. *Call after Midnight*, a romantic thriller, was followed
by eight more romantic suspense novels. She also wrote a screenplay,
Adrift, which aired as a 1993 CBS Movie of the Week.

Gerritsen's first medical thriller, *Harvest*, was released in 1996, and
it marked her debut on the *New York Times* bestseller list. Her suspense
novels since then include *Gravity* and *Playing with Fire*, among others.
Her books have been published in forty countries, and more than 30 million copies have been sold around the world. Her series of crime novels
featuring homicide detective Jane Rizzoli and medical examiner Maura
Isles inspired the hit television series *Rizzoli & Isles*, starring Angie
Harmon and Sasha Alexander. Now retired from medicine, Gerritsen
writes full-time and lives in Maine.

[Thank You, Teacher]

[He Made Class Fun]

ALISON HAISLIP
actor

NICHOLAS BURO
science, Voorhees High School, Glen Gardner, New Jersey

I ALWAYS LOVED SCIENCE and was a great science student. I probably could have become an engineer, or a research scientist, or possibly even an astronaut. So how ironic is it that my favorite science teacher is the reason I never pursued a job in science?

Nicholas Buro was my science teacher at Voorhees High School in Glen Gardner, New Jersey, twice: once for honors chemistry during my sophomore year and again the following year for AP physics. He was one of those teachers who made class fun. He was always laughing, always joking, making sure we had plenty of hands-on experiments, but best of all, he wasn't a pushover. He kept the class orderly because he understood that in a classroom filled with explosive chemicals and heavy pulleys and weights, getting too lax with the fun could lead to an unsafe environment. I greatly respected that he always had a sense of humor while keeping everyone in line.

I may be bragging a bit, but I believe Mr. Buro considered

me one of his best students. He affectionately called me "kid," and we would crack jokes with each other during class because of our similar brand of sarcasm. Because of this, he became a sort of confidant for me. So it wasn't surprising when, halfway through my junior year, I went to him while I was struggling with college applications. Being a good student, I luckily had a lot of options when it came to what I wanted to do after high school. The problem was, I hadn't decided yet, and most college applications wanted you to list your major.

Again, I loved science. But I also loved singing. And acting. And performing in general. I had been a part both of the school and of the community theater performances, as well as part of every choir and band my school had to offer, since I was eight. It was my life. But when you're a straight-A student and graduating near the top of your class, telling people you wanted to go into show business was frowned upon. So I was struggling with the decision that every artist has to struggle with at some point: Do I follow my dreams and passions into a very unstable but possibly very gratifying career? Or do I play it safe and get into something I know I can do and I know I'm very good at and would probably be quite successful doing?

When I came to Mr. Buro with this question, I'll never forget what he said:

"Alison, you're great at science. But you *love* acting."

It was because of that single conversation that I decided to pursue my dreams. I went on to study theater arts at Boston College, moved to Los Angeles three weeks after I graduated, and have had an amazing career and extremely fun-filled life for the past ten years.

Sadly, Mr. Buro passed away, completely unexpectedly, a few years after I graduated from high school. He was in his late forties and contracted lung cancer, even though he had never smoked and was an active runner. It breaks my heart to know I'll never be able to thank him personally for the impact he had on my life, but I know if he could see me now, he'd give me a playful punch on the arm and say, "Good job, kid. Now don't get cocky."

ALISON HAISLIP was a series regular in Hulu's first original scripted series entitled *Battleground*, produced by Marc Webb, as well as a host for Hulu's daily show *The Morning After*. You can find her on Geek & Sundry's RPG show, *Titansgrave*, with Wil Wheton. She also hosted what was dubbed the *Chelsea Lately* for nerds, *Four Points with Alex Albrecht* on Chris Hardwick's Nerdist network, and was Hardwick's correspondent for his show *The Nerdist* on BBCA, as well as the correspondent for Zac Levi's innovative company, Nerd Machine, which covers all things geek. While Haislip is well-known from her past duties on G4's *Attack of the Show* and *American Ninja Warrior*, she garnered a lot of attention when she took on the innovative role of the first ever on-air Social Media Correspondent on *The Voice* during its first season. Haislip's other television credits include *Shameless*, *Bones*, *NCIS*, *Franklin & Bash*, and *Reno 911!*, and she has a recurring role in *Con Man* with Alan Tudyk and Nathan Fillion.

STEWART LEWIS

writer and singer

MR. POTTS

English, Dover-Sherborn High School, Dover, Massachusetts

AT A RECENT DINNER a friend asked me if I could name the Best Actor or Best Actress from the Oscars two years earlier. Even though I consider myself pop-culture savvy, I was completely at a loss. Then he said, "Okay, now give me the name of a teacher who inspired you." Immediately, the name came out.

"Mr. Potts."

"And he somehow changed your life, right?"

I thought about it for a second, and then nodded.

"The power of teachers is overlooked and underestimated in so many ways," my friend said. "There is too much emphasis on celebrity."

Mr. Potts *was* a celebrity — to me. I remember walking into ninth-grade English class expecting to see a geeky old guy in a plaid shirt, shapeless pants, and brown Posturepedic shoes. Instead, Mr. Potts looked like a hip older brother: curly hair shagged out, a silver bracelet, and boot-cut jeans (it was a casual Friday in 1985). As he told us about himself, his hands danced to the sound of his words, and his lively eyes locked into the eyes of each and every one of us.

When the class clown indirectly called him a hippie, Mr. Potts replied, "Better than a Republican," not missing a beat.

He handed out some books and had us all introduce ourselves, and then we went over the syllabus. At the end of the class he held up an album cover with a photograph of a man washed with light.

"One more thing. Your homework for this weekend is to go out and pick up a copy of Peter Gabriel's new album, *So*. If you don't have the money, steal it." Some kids laughed.

"This album," he said with a sweep of his big hand, "will change the face of rock and roll."

We all were dumbfounded but wrote down the assignment.

That afternoon my mother dragged me along to her aerobics class, which was very in at the time. I sat on the sidelines and gazed at the women, thankful that my mother didn't look like them: teased hair and caked-on makeup. Mom was more au natural, and it made me proud. As we were leaving I pulled her into Strawberries Music, explaining to her about my English assignment, and though skeptical, she complied. The clerk was just taking the records and tapes out of the boxes. He looked at me like I was a rock star for even knowing about it. I decided right then that Mr. Potts was super cool.

That night after dinner I put the cassette into my Walkman and sat on my porch as the last bit of sun warmed the sloping hills behind our house. The opening track, "Red Rain," was like a musical blanket, covering me in a dreamy soundscape that slowed my heart and tingled my feet. I couldn't take the headphones off, and just flipped the tape over and over again. The eighth track, "In Your Eyes," would soon become a number one hit and the theme song to the classic John Cusack flick *Say Anything*, a quintessential movie of my high school years from which I am still able to recite scenes from memory.

I took the Walkman into bed with me. When my mother peeked in to say good night, she said, "Who is this teacher again?"

That Monday we all had our cassettes and albums in our backpacks, along with our notebooks. I didn't realize until much later the effect the music had on me — certainly more than a textbook ever would.

The next day he asked us how we felt about the record. One kid said he thought it was "stupid," and another said, "[It was] cool but I don't see what it has to do with English." I raised my hand and said what I had rehearsed on the bus ride to school: "dramatic and sensual." Some of the other kids looked at me funny, but I didn't care. When Mr. Potts said, "Now we're getting somewhere," I felt on top of the world.

I should tell you that all my life I had been playing music. My parents were in a bluegrass band, and when I was five somebody threw me a tambourine. I went on to play drums, then guitar, and I had even written a few folk songs. Until then my heroes had been Crosby, Stills & Nash. This Peter Gabriel thing was a whole different story. Today my songs have been featured on TV, in film, and distributed worldwide, and I partly have Mr. Potts to thank for that — not just because of that first assignment, but because he was the first person to instill in me the power of possibility, the virtue of diversity, and the courage to step outside the lines that were drawn for me.

I began to look forward to his class. One day, when the lights were out in the room, I panicked, thinking he was absent, or there was a field trip I didn't know about. But when I entered, I saw that there was a TV set up and paper bowls filled with popcorn. He told us that our next assignment was to write a paper on our reaction to the movie we were about to watch, *The Graduate*.

When I think back on it, Mr. Potts most likely wasn't allowed to show us a movie with such content, but he wasn't a man with boundaries. He was probably the type of teacher that had a stash of marijuana somewhere in his house for special occasions, or once followed the Grateful Dead, maybe even toyed with bisexuality. Anyway, at least it wasn't *Caligula*.

I was fascinated by Anne Bancroft, and loved the use of Simon and Garfunkel songs, and though my paper was poorly edited, it had a passion that Mr. Potts took to. He gave me a B-plus.

Mr. Potts never seemed too fazed by what anyone said about him. He seemed to take the good with the bad and to try to learn from every situation. When a smart-ass challenged him, he challenged back. When an outcast ignored him, he figured out a way to get on her level. He'd make up games that everyone could get involved in, and it was in Mr. Potts's class that you found yourself making connections with students from groups you would never associate with outside those doors. He was a catalyst. But most important, he *cared*. Not just for his paycheck, which even as ninth graders we knew wasn't much, but his desire to influence us seemed inherent, like it was what he was born to do. Leave a mark. Even the ones who refused to let him in felt it.

In my sophomore year I was captain of the tennis team, and Mr. Potts was the assistant coach. Halfway through the season, the head coach became ill, so Mr. Potts took over. He was unpredictable and a bit silly, but that is not to say he wasn't tough. He would work us like crazy — on the court and in class. But it was worth it. He was someone from whom you wanted to gain trust.

Since I was the captain, a lot of times I had to play Mr. Potts in singles during practice. Our levels were basically the same, although he was stronger than I was and obviously had more experience. By the end of our sets I would be panting, my tongue hanging out like a golden retriever's. He was so competitive, and I had never fought as hard for anything as I did in those matches. It was always neck and neck, and he would usually win. But once, at the end of the season, I won in a tiebreaker. Thinking back, I realize he most likely let me win at the last moment, but at the time I was so proud I almost cried. And as he shook my hand I could have sworn I saw a glint of a tear in his eye too.

For my senior project I recorded a demo on a four-track. I covered the song "After Midnight," and as all the teachers walked around to everyone's presentation, I kept waiting for Mr. Potts. When he finally came around, my heart beat in triplets as he put the headphones on and listened.

"Nice new take on a classic song," he said. "I like the syncopated guitar work. Good one, Captain."

At graduation he gave me a cigar and a mixed tape. I gave the cigar to my dad, but I would still be playing the mix if cassette players hadn't become obsolete.

I didn't see him again until about five years later. I was boarding a ferry to Martha's Vineyard and I heard a voice behind me say, "How's your tennis game keeping up?" There was Mr. Potts, still tan and shaggy with a sparkle in his eye, as if no time had gone by.

"I'm a little rusty," I said.

I was traveling with some girls, and after we had caught up a bit, he asked, "One of them your girlfriend?"

At that point, I had been out as gay for a couple of years, and comfortable around most of my friends, but not really out to my family. I had always been wary of that inevitable question, and the awkward remark that usually followed: a cast-off, or a lie, or nothing at all, which only seemed to make it more obvious.

He looked at me and registered the apprehension in my eyes.

"Hey," he said and patted my shoulder, "I get it. I think I got it before you did."

I smiled and said, "Well, that was easy."

Later, during the boat ride, he brought me a can of beer. We chatted about old times and once again, he made me feel like I was the center of the universe.

When we arrived, a friend asked me who "that guy" was. I didn't know whether to say my teacher or my friend, and what came to me was "He's one of those people who change your life."

STEWART LEWIS is the author of the young adult novels *The Secret Ingredient* and *You Have Seven Messages*. His books have been translated into five languages. He is also a singer-songwriter and radio personality. For more information, check out www.stewartlewis.com.

[Thank God for English Teachers]

JOHN ROSENGREN
author

ROGER MAHN
journalism, Wayzata High School, Wayzata, Minnesota

BY MY SENIOR YEAR IN HIGH SCHOOL, my drinking and drugging had loomed into addiction. I got busted at a party, got locked up in detox, and eventually landed in treatment. Eventually, I got sober.

At seventeen I had to start over. I had been a popular partier, a cocky kid with a quick wit and a smart mouth. That had all been a schtick to cover up the pain and confusion and loneliness of adolescence. Without dope, I felt raw, vulnerable, and exposed. Who was I? What would I be?

Thank God for English teachers. Roger Mahn, my journalism teacher during my senior year, spotted what he deemed talent in the sports columns I scratched out for the student newspaper, and he took a personal interest in me. During an independent study with him that year, the conversation in our one-on-one sessions was more likely to turn toward growing as a person than revising a lead paragraph. That's the way he was with all the students: encouraging them to risk being themselves. He cared about us as people first, and we could tell.

For me, it worked. Roger — as we called him — helped me stay sober my senior year. He kindled an interest in writing. And he inspired me to teach. Without his support and influence, my life not only wouldn't have been the same, but it might not have even been anymore.

John Rosengren is an award-winning freelance journalist and author. He has written for the *Atlantic*, the *New Yorker*, *Men's Journal*, *Reader's Digest*, and *Sports Illustrated*, among other publications. He has taught English literature, journalism, and creative writing at St. Thomas Academy, Newbury College, Boston University, and the University of Minnesota. Visit him at www.johnrosengren.net.

[I Am Thankful for Her Efforts]

TOMMY JAMES
singer-songwriter

BARBARA KIETZER, typing,
MISS KANE, math,
Niles High School, Niles, Michigan

BARBARA KIETZER, my typing teacher, was very supportive in all my efforts in school, not just in her class. She took an interest in my desire to be a musician and gave me the confidence to stick with it. Of course, the typing did not hurt since I use the same method when I work on my computer! We are still close friends, and I visit with her whenever I go back to Michigan.

Then there is Miss Kane, my math teacher. I am thankful for her efforts to get me through a subject that I wasn't too interested in; however, I realize now how important math is. I can read and understand my financial documents, royalty statements, and other financial situations pertaining to my career.

TOMMY JAMES is an American pop-rock musician, singer, songwriter, and record producer, widely known as the leader of the 1960s rock band Tommy James and the Shondells. On the road, he and his Shondells are still rockin', performing their many timeless hits to sellout crowds across the country. When not on the road, James continues to craft new music geared toward film and television and to develop new business opportunities for his company, Aura Entertainment Group.

I'M A TEACHER MYSELF, and I do think there's something to the notion that education is a sacred profession. At least that's what I think now. At the age of fourteen I was bitterly disappointed in education. That year my father died, and we moved from suburban San Francisco back to a small town in Wisconsin. I say "back" because we were from Wisconsin originally. We'd moved to California only because my father had been transferred there by his company, and now he was dead, and with him any possible reason for staying on the West Coast. Or so went the thinking of the rest of my family.

I hated the idea. I liked California. I liked San Francisco. I liked cities. I liked my enormous 2,500-student Los Altos High, with its theater classes and music program and history teacher who was reported to be a communist and my friends who I'd gone to junior high school with. I liked pretty much all of it.

My mother bought an old farm outside De Pere, Wisconsin, and I went to East De Pere High, where the largest club was the Future Farmers of America, and there was no theater program, and football was a religion. I had nothing but contempt for the teachers and students alike, all of whom I considered rubes. I wasn't so far-off, actually, but that's another story. My English teacher that sophomore year was Mrs. Ziemann. It didn't occur to me to scorn her. She was too likable for that, but I was already in the habit of challenging my teachers, questioning them, correcting them, and being a general pain in the ass. It made me feel better. What can I say? I was fourteen and unhappy.

Whenever I sensed an opening, I pounced: I quibbled over word usage and correction of pronunciation. I insisted, for example, that *err* be pronounced "ur" not "er" (they're both correct); that "punkin" was the only correct way to say *pumpkin* (either is fine); that the correct word was *empathic* and not *empathetic* (ditto); and that *disinterested* and *uninterested* had entirely different meanings. I was sort of right with the last one, but being right wasn't the point. I could usually intimidate the teacher, who was generally caught off guard and couldn't be absolutely sure I wasn't right.

I was insufferable.

Sometimes my strategy was to ask a question that might trip up the teacher. I would ask anything, no matter how obscure, no matter how trivial or pointless. Sometimes the teacher could answer, of course, which was fine. But often I could catch them in the act of being ignorant and make them squirm.

One day, in the middle of reading *Julius Caesar* aloud in class, it was Mrs. Ziemann's turn. I looked at the lines of versified dialogue on the page before me. I had never read Shakespeare before. (Despite my precocious attitude I was actually incredibly ignorant.) I noticed that when one character stopped speaking in the middle of a line of verse, the next character's line began at that same point on the page. It wasn't justified left. I was confused about that. More to the point, I hoped Mrs. Ziemann would be confused. So I asked her why the lines were laid out like that.

She looked right at me, and she said, "You know, I have no idea. I'll have to ask one of the other teachers, and I'll get back to you."

And she did.

It was at that moment that I realized what education was about. That we're all learning, all the time, and that to admit ignorance is simply to admit the truth. There's so much we don't know. Why not just say so?

Mrs. Ziemann became Shirley after graduation, and we've been good friends ever since. I don't know that I've ever told her that her answer that day was the beginning of my own career as a teacher. But now I think I may have to.

STUART SPENCER is the author of *The Playwright's Guidebook*, as well as numerous plays that have been produced across the country and the world. He also teaches playwriting, theater history, and dramaturgy at Sarah Lawrence College.

GILLIAN ANDERSON

actor

MS. BABCOCK

English, City High Middle School, Grand Rapids, Michigan

WHEN I WAS IN HIGH SCHOOL, I was a bit lost for a while. My grades were bad, my attention was worse, and my feelings about school in general were heading me in a southern direction. Enter a teacher named Sharon Babcock, who not only taught us English the way kids want to learn it, with an appreciation for words, an excitement for language, and a curiosity about literature, but also encouraged us to write creatively. The safe environment she created enabled me to write from my deepest places and, I have no doubt, helped me shed some of the angst that had been building through those complicated teenager years. A high point in my relationship with Ms. Babcock was when she visited me in in-house detention to help me with a poem I was struggling with. Not only did she show me that I was worth showing up for no matter what, but she also liked what I wrote and encouraged me to keep going...keep going with my poetry and keep going in life, an encouragement that has stayed with me into adulthood and that I still rely on when I feel like giving up.

Thank you, Ms. Babcock. And thank you, Bruce, for inspiring your wife to organize this book, which led me to remember Ms. Babcock, but most of all, thank you for inspiring your classrooms. Whether or not your students appreciate you now, whether or not they look back in gratitude in the years to come, the gift you *have* is that you can wake up every day with a clear conscience and know in your deepest places that you are doing the right thing. That's all that really matters at the end of the day. You can fill your heart with that.

GILLIAN ANDERSON gained worldwide recognition for her role in *The X-Files*, garnering awards and critical praise over the show's nine-year run. Other notable credits include *The House of Mirth*, BBC's *Great Expectations*, *The Last King of Scotland*, and the acclaimed miniseries *Bleak House*. Her stage role in *A Streetcar Named Desire* won her an Evening Standard Theatre Award for her performance as Blanche Du Bois. Her most recent film roles include Kate in *Robot Overlords*, opposite Sir Ben Kingsley, and she will be playing Edwina Mountbatten to Hugh Bonneville's Lord Mountbatten in Gurinda Chada's *Viceroy's House*. Recent TV credits include NBC's *Hannibal*, the BBC2 series *The Fall*, and the BBC/Weinstein production of *War and Peace*.

[In a Different Way]

FAYE KELLERMAN
author

MR. PATTON, MR. CARRINGTON, MR. JACOBS
Grant High School, Valley Glen, California

EVEN THOUGH I AM A PROFESSIONAL WRITER, I was a math major in high school.

One of the reasons for this was three of my high school math teachers whom I adored — Mr. Patton, Mr. Carrington, and Mr. Jacobs. Each influenced me in a different way. Mr. Patton was a jokester, Mr. Carrington was a punster, and Mr. Jacobs was an obsessive-compulsive. His printing was neater than a typewriter, but he was such a kind man and had such a big influence that I began to try to emulate his printing. As a result, I had the neatest, most legible notes around. Everyone wanted to copy them.

I had a chance to see Mr. Jacobs again when I was given an award by my high school. I finally got a chance to tell him what a wonderful influence he was on me. All three were so kind to me at a time when I was at my most vulnerable. Not by being shrinky or overly attentive — just by being wonderful people. I could laugh with them, and they spurred me on to a more meaningful experience. As a result I was a math major in college. Teachers don't realize the long-term effects they have on students. Mine taught me what it means for an outsider to care.

FAYE KELLERMAN is a *New York Times*–bestselling author of mystery novels. Her books include the Peter Decker/Rina Lazarus series as well as the novels *The Quality of Mercy*, *Moon Music*, and *Straight into Darkness*. She has cowritten two novels with her husband, Jonathan Kellerman, and cowritten a young adult novel with her daughter, Aliza, entitled *Prism*.

JOHN WHALEN
poet

RODNEY JONES
English, Greenville High School, Greenville, Tennessee

AT THE END OF THE SUMMER between junior and senior year, a new teacher called. His name was Rodney Jones, he said, never Mr. Jones, even from the start. Did I want to join him and his wife and some of my classmates, if he could convince them, to see the Artrain thirty miles away in Johnson City? My English teacher had told him I wrote poetry. I didn't know who this man on the phone was, and I certainly didn't know what an Artrain was. Forty-one years later, I can't guess why I said yes. Yet I'm glad every day that I did. Risking a potentially awkward evening with unfamiliar people gained me a new friend and a lifelong engagement with writing. The Artrain was pretty interesting too, an art gallery, a poetry reading, and a juggling show all wrapped into one. Who were these artists, anyway? It seemed they all had a different way of thinking.

I was mostly interested in science and math at that time and had just returned from a National Science Foundation summer program for high school students at Bennett College in Greensboro, North Carolina. In junior year I had taken physics with kids a year ahead of me and was disappointed that our school didn't offer calculus. I remember writing poems that spring, poems for a certain girl and later for another girl. Poems that contained emotion without craft. I remember trips to the library to find poetry, mostly written by Rod McKuen, who was hugely popular then. I remember perching in the window seat of a very warm dorm room at Bennett College as I daydreamed of reading my own poems to a vast and appreciative audience. As a famous poet, I'd live on the coast (I'd been to Myrtle Beach once with my best friend and his family) and spend my days watching the waves curl and break against the sand. The truth was, though, one didn't turn to Rod McKuen for substance or depth. No real work was being done in his poems, not with language or imagery or deep emotion. In other words, I had no lasting connection to poetry and would have given up on it in quick order, gone on to something else. After all, I was about to have a girlfriend for the first time and a dishwashing job on weekends at a busy steak house. Because of Rodney, because of his infectious excitement about the possibilities of poetry, I never did give up on writing; I never wanted to.

Rodney Jones was an extraordinary teacher who recognized and encouraged the potential for creativity in me and all his students. He taught in our sleepy east Tennessee school district as a poet in the National Endowment for the Arts Artists-in-the-Schools program. Soft-spoken, but confident and intellectually rigorous, he was interested in everything. He was different from the other teachers. We had seen long hair before but not on a teacher. Rodney's hair was a nimbus of dark curls above a tweed jacket or, in colder weather, a tan leather coat. Two or three hours a week a few of us were permitted to leave English period to write and talk about poetry with Rodney in a borrowed classroom. Working with him was not a passive learning experience. As much as his teaching style was low-key, it was also effective. He didn't lecture. He discussed. He listened. He was fundamentally curious — about us and our untried talents, about his own writing, what he could do with language, how well he could craft it.

To help us avoid clichés and worn habits of expression, at first he had us write only sentences we had never heard before. We needed to learn to trust our own voices. He encouraged us to write from our own perspective, not from that of other writers or based on ideas on how we *should* write. He treated us as if we understood what he was revealing to us. He claimed ideas and language were alive, that they mattered. From his personal library, he gave us books of contemporary American poets, men and women who in previous decades had broken all the molds. They wrote about anything and everything. They did so with grace and style and energy. Suddenly, language and literature, poetry especially, were not dusty carcasses of stilted rhyme and meter. Rather, they were painfully, wonderfully relevant. With poetry, if you worked hard, if you were good enough to get away with it, you could say almost anything, express the most complex emotions, maybe even describe the fuzzy architectures that underpin consciousness itself. You could describe an emotion, tie it to a leaf, a murder of crows, a deaf girl playing. You could talk to your own soul, it turned out. And if it talked back, you could write that down too.

Rodney offered positive feedback and detailed suggestions as we labored over our writing. He challenged us to bring our best, most well-crafted poems and to work even harder to make them better. In our poems he would find the two or three verses that contained some music, some depth. Cut away the rest, he told us. Keep this part and start again. Craft was nearly everything. He pushed us to write and to read. To read everything. For free, for the cost of paying attention, he shared his incredible passion and an advanced, critical understanding of poetry. He cracked open the world of art for me, a discovery from which I have yet to recover. He didn't give me a voice, but he listened to the one I had and helped me understand that by sheer attention and sustained work I could make it more genuine and more original, more mine.

In the anthology of student work he put together for us, Rodney introduced the collection by saying, "If words were clothes, perhaps most of us would be dressed in blue serge with dark ties and gray jackets. It is not that other combinations do not occur to us, only that we are either too lazy to experiment, or, realizing the risk involved in mixing colors more imaginatively, we decide to play it safe, to trust the neutral blues and grays." Following his advice, I have always bet on the brighter colors.

JOHN WHALEN was born in Michigan, grew up in Tennessee, and lives now in Spokane, Washington. He has been writing poetry since 1974. While making a living outside academia — as a printer, a computer salesperson, and for the past many years as a computer security consultant — he has also taught writing to students from elementary-school age to college age to senior citizens in a psychiatric center. Whalen is the author of a poetry collection, *Caliban*, and two chapbooks, *Above the Pear Trees* and *In Honor of the Spigot*.

[Forty Years Later]

DAN MILLMAN
author

MR. THOMPSON
English, John Marshall High School, Los Angeles, California

QUITE AN ODD THING HAPPENED TO ME while I was deeply immersed in writing a recent book, *The Journeys of Socrates*. I had been writing for nearly a year and was almost finished with the first draft when the thought came to me: I should write to my high school English teacher, Mr. Thompson.

I could still remember my first day in Mr. Thompson's class. I noticed that he had had surgery for a cleft upper lip and palate, and bore a scar, along with a difficulty articulating certain words. Yet he took great care to enunciate — a care that would carry over to all that he taught, all that he did.

We studied Thornton Wilder's play *Our Town* and the novel *Mutiny on the Bounty*. That I recall these specific literary works after forty years is a testament to Mr. Thompson's enthusiasm and power to draw us deeply into the history, drama, and humanity of such classic stories. He was also a Civil War buff and often hilarious raconteur, going into depth on subjects that others might gloss over.

But this is only the beginning of the story. Let's jump ahead forty years. I had not thought of him all that time, but here it was — this persistent urge to write him a letter. So I pushed away from the keyboard, picked up the phone, and called my old high school in Los Angeles, where I was informed that they didn't keep old records; I'd have to call the Board of Education. I did so, and explained to the person in records that I wanted to write to Mr. Thompson, my tenth-grade English teacher.

"We have many Thompsons," she said. "What's his first name?"

"His first name? Umm...*Mister?*" I half-joked before remembering that his first name was Irwin. I provided this information.

"Well, we can't give you private information," she finally told me, "but if you send the letter to him, care of my office, I'll do my best to see that it gets forwarded."

So I wrote a brief letter, telling Mr. Thompson about my career as an author, and expressing my deep appreciation to him for his guidance and inspiration. I credited him with igniting that spark in me that became a love of writing, and told him that he had certainly inspired — and changed the lives of — many students over his many years of teaching.

I had no idea whether the letter would reach him or if he was even still alive. But I sealed the letter, put it in the mail, and turned back to working on my book.

About three weeks later, I received a return letter in the mail. It wasn't from Mr. Thompson, but from his daughter, grown into a teacher herself. She wrote to tell me that her father, Irwin Thompson, had read my letter in bed just two days before he died. She wanted me to know that he cried when he read my words, and that they read the letter at his memorial soon after.

How could I have guessed that those few words, that simple impulse to contact him just before he died, would have had such an impact? I knew that many hundreds of other students had also been inspired and energized by his example and his teaching. Perhaps I had written for us all.

I hold teachers, and the life education they provide, in high regard. For years we had a poster on our wall that said, "What if the schools had all the money they needed and the government had to hold a bake sale to buy a bomber?" The service that teachers provide is as important as the work of surgeons or attorneys or engineers. What work is more important than serving as mentors to our children?

All of us can recall one or two teachers who stand out, as Mr. Thompson had stood out for me — teachers who saw a potential in us that we did not yet see in ourselves; teachers who made loving demands on us to grow, learn, rise to the occasion.

We owe a debt of gratitude to all our teachers. It is a debt I can never fully repay, but that won't stop me from trying.

DAN MILLMAN, a former world champion athlete, university coach, and college professor, is the author of *Way of the Peaceful Warrior*, now a major motion picture. His fourteen books have inspired millions of readers in twenty-nine languages. Millman also speaks worldwide. For more information, visit www.peacefulwarrior.com.

[Respect]

BEAU BRIDGES
actor

CLINTON DEWITT NYE
public speaking, Venice High School, Los Angeles, California

ONE OF MY FAVORITE TEACHERS in high school was Clinton Dewitt Nye, at Venice High School. His class was public speaking, but it was really a place where his students could talk about everything having to do with life. He had a great sense of humor. The first day of class he had a strange-looking doll he called "a nebbish" tacked onto the ceiling. He asked us to think about what the doll represented and told us we would discuss it at the end of the year. He said that to him it represented a strike against the establishment.

When he gave us our final grades, he walked to each student's desk and wrote their grade in their report card. He gave my friend sitting in front of me an A. Then he gave me a C. My friend laughed, which prompted Mr. Nye to take my friend's report card back, and he crossed out the A and gave him a C. He then took my report card, crossed out the C and gave me an A. I guess having respect meant more to him then scholastic performance.

BEAU BRIDGES is an actor-director, father, husband, and youth athletic coach. He has starred in numerous movies, including *The Fabulous Baker Boys*, *Max Payne*, and *Jerry McGuire*. He has won three Emmys, two Golden Globes, and one Grammy.

[A "Class Act"]

ROY FIRESTONE
sportscaster

JAY JENSEN
drama, Miami Beach High School, Miami Beach, Florida

JAY JENSEN WAS MY DRAMA TEACHER in high school. I say "my" because everyone felt he was "theirs." Jay also taught men like actors Andy Garcia and Mickey Rourke, and director Brett Ratner.

He called himself the "teacher to the stars," but he was the biggest star. We didn't know it, because he guarded his private life, but Jay was worth about $15 million. He worked two jobs, teaching drama to kids from all walks of life and taking us to perform at nursing homes and economically disadvantaged areas. He never said a word about the money.

He was a very eccentric man. A documentary was made about him called, fittingly, *Class Act*. Jay was a mentor, a friend, and my biggest fan.

In late 2006 he was diagnosed with prostate cancer, and he fought hard, even making it to his film's premiere in Hollywood. What I got from that film, and his life, was simple. Money is important, and God knows teachers don't see a lot of it. But working your passion, sharing it, and passing on what you know and love to someone else is one of life's greatest deeds. It's more important than money.

Jay Jensen passed away in early 2007, and I owe so much to him.

ROY FIRESTONE is a critically acclaimed broadcast journalist who has won seven Emmys and seven Cable ACE Awards. He has interviewed more than five thousand people, including nearly every major sports figure. Firestone performs his multimedia review before audiences in Las Vegas and at major sporting events, meetings, formal events, and conventions throughout the world.

ERIC LIEBETRAU

editor

MRS. WATKINS

English, Wando High School, Mt. Pleasant, South Carolina

IT'S ODD TO THINK that my reading life began with the Smashing Pumpkins — my *adult* reading and writing life, that is, beyond Dr. Seuss, Hardy Boys adventures, Encyclopedia Brown mysteries, and *Calvin and Hobbes* collections. "Porcelina of the Vast Oceans," Billy Corgan's dreamlike portrait from the 1995 album *Mellon Collie and the Infinite Sadness*, proved to be the catalyst for one of the more memorable writing experiences of my life:

> As far as you take me, that's where I believe.
> The realm of soft delusions, floating on the leaves.
> On a distant shoreline, she waves her arms to me.
> As all the thought police, are closing in for sleep.

That's how the dream opens, launching a journey of shimmering, magical images and anthemic music. And that's where Mrs. Watkins, my tenth-grade English teacher, comes in, and where my journey with books and literature really took off.

When I stepped into her class the first day of my sophomore year, I had no idea that this pleasant, ordinary-looking woman would be largely responsible for changing the way I viewed life and its connection to literature. As part of her unit on Romanticism — that sprawling eighteenth-century artistic and literary movement personified, at least in literature, by William Blake, Samuel Taylor Coleridge, and William Wordsworth — Mrs. Watkins included an assignment that would pique the interest of nearly any fifteen-year-old mind: Choose a piece of music that embodies Romantic ideals, and explain why.

As we delved deeper into the Romantic poets, I was particularly struck by Blake and Coleridge. Only later would I read Blake's masterpiece *The Marriage of Heaven and Hell*, but for the time being, I was enchanted by the muscular power of "The Tyger," the boundless adventure of "The Rime of the Ancient Mariner," and the hallucinatory swirl of "Kubla Khan."

At the same time, I was discovering the transformative power of rock, especially Led Zeppelin. The day Mrs. Watkins assigned the Romanticism essay, I started combing through Zeppelin lyrics, many of which were inspired by ancient magic and fantastical elements in the vein of J. R. R. Tolkien. "Stairway to Heaven" seemed the obvious choice, but to a fifteen-year-old, it was far too cliché for my purposes. After rejecting "The Battle of Evermore," "Misty Mountain Hop," and "Over the Hills and Far Away," in addition to countless others I can no longer recall, I decided that maybe Zeppelin wasn't the way to go — the lyrics were too dark, too overtly sexual, and, despite my newly found teen angst, perhaps too primal for a tenth-grade assignment.

Luckily, the Smashing Pumpkins released *Mellon Collie* in

fall 1995, and I could tell on my first listen that this album had at least one track that I could defend as "Romantic," with a capital R — and there she was, Porcelina:

In the slipstream, of thoughtless thoughts
The light of all that's good, the light of all that's true
To the fringes gladly, I walk unadorned
With gods and their creations
With filth and disease
Porcelina, she waits for me there
With seashell hissing lullabyes
And whispers fathomed deep inside my own
Hidden thoughts and alibis
My secret thoughts come alive

It was all there: the reverence of nature; elusive, ethereal imagery; the significance of intuition and feelings over rational thought; the pastoral as more important than the urban; Wordsworth's famous definition of good poetry as the "spontaneous overflow of personal feelings." It even reflected much of the criticism Romanticism endured as being too dreamlike, too flowery. Corgan was known for occasionally floating off into the atmosphere, but so were the Romantic poets. It was the connection I made between the two that demonstrated to me the power of both art forms—and the cross-pollination of thought that can result from using one to contextualize and analyze the other.

Fortunately, I got an A-plus on my essay, but more important, that assignment truly sparked my love for the written word — reading it, writing it, analyzing it, and deconstructing it. Now, thirteen years later, my fascination with music and literature has expanded exponentially.

Teachers constantly struggle with methods to engage their students in learning. Sometimes all it takes is a simple assignment that uses existing teenage interests as a tool to explore curriculum-based learning and beyond. I have Mrs. Watkins to thank for igniting that interest in me, an interest that informs nearly every aspect of my life today.

ERIC LIEBETRAU is the managing editor and nonfiction editor of *Kirkus Reviews*. He is a member of the board of directors for the National Book Critics Circle, and he contributes book reviews, music reviews, and other literary and cultural features to a variety of national publications, including *People*, the *New Yorker*, the *Boston Globe*, and *Charleston City Paper*.

["That" Teacher]

WAYNE FEDERMAN
actor and comedian

PHILIP BEASLEY
American history, South Plantation High School, Plantation, Florida

PHILIP BEASLEY, South Plantation High School; he was *that* teacher.

I spent two years in his class and, honestly, it didn't really matter what the course title was (for me, American history and psychology). Beasley was there to teach his students to think creatively. That was his mission.

Other teachers taught a curriculum — facts, words, theorems, skills. Beasley added a context — a framework for understanding. He always preached the power of dreams. He demonstrated how *everything* created or achieved by human beings, be it the US Constitution, a water park, the four-minute mile, or the hydrogen bomb, was once just a spark, an idea.

Sure, we learned about the Battle of the Bulge and Pavlov's dog, but the primary lesson was the potential of your mind. Paul McCartney, he told us, composed the tune "Yesterday" in his sleep. Same with Keith Richards and the riff to "Satisfaction." Seriously, in their *sleep*. I never had a teacher like that before.

Every session fit neatly into this view. The Founding Fathers *dreamed* of living in a land without paying taxes to a king. That is how history was made. And, just as important, that is how your life, your history, will unfold: first, in your mind.

For extra credit in psychology he recommended we keep a dream journal. He told us that we must begin writing the moment we woke up. Of course I liked to sleep as late as possible (I ran to school unshowered and without breakfast for years), so that was extra credit I never received. I completed another Beasley project instead, the "treasure map," a collage of what you wanted your life to become. I pasted together a photomontage of George Carlin, Milton Berle, Jerry Lee Lewis, Victor Borge, Woody Allen, Richard Pryor, and a dozen other comedians performing onstage.

We were a nondefined generation — stuck between the Vietnam-era baby boomers and the Gen Xers. The popular word to describe us was *apathetic*. It was a concept that Beasley railed against. He would exploit any subject to spark a debate or provoke new concepts. Nothing was off-limits.

Florida law required him to teach one semester of a minicourse called Americanism vs. Communism. Beasley argued for the Reds — not because he leaned that way, but because he wanted us to be able to *appreciate and articulate* the benefits of a representative republic. It was important to him that we could be advocates.

He was democracy personified. American history was first period and, on the very first day, he asked the class what *we thought* the punishment should be for student tardiness. We debated and voted on it. The majority ruled.

Beasley was tremendously encouraging and nurturing of my artistic ambitions. Some of my earliest comedy bits were performed, standing on top of his desk, in American history class. At the time I did a Kaufman-esque (Andy, not George S.) Elvis Presley impression. He allowed his classroom to become a comedy club — to help me.

Twenty-five years after graduation I went back to visit Beasley. I asked him if teaching had changed for him. Was the year-after-year *Groundhog Day* aspect of his job wearing him down? He agreed that it was different, that the majority of his time was now spent on discipline. Teaching was not as fun for him.

I'm not convinced we were any more disciplined. After all, Beasley was still a young man (twenty-seven) when he taught us, brimming with new ideas and energy. Some days he walked us out of the building, across Peter's Road, and had class in the park — just to shake things up. Of course, I will always see him as that twenty-seven-year-old, with his mischievous grin and flop of brown hair. He was like Peck's bad boy.

I lead my life as he once suggested: skeptical but never cynical. And thirty years later, in a very real way, I still stand on Philip Beasley's desk.

WAYNE FEDERMAN is a stand-up comedian, actor, comedy writer, and author who has performed on *The Tonight Show* and *Late Night with Jimmy Fallon*. He has appeared in more than fifty movies and TV shows, including *The 40-Year-Old Virgin*, *Legally Blonde*, *50 First Dates*, *Knocked Up*, *Step Brothers*, *The X-Files*, *Curb Your Enthusiasm*, *New Girl*, *Community*, and *Shameless*. He was also the head monologue writer for *Late Night with Jimmy Fallon* and coauthored a bestselling sports biography on "Pistol Pete" Maravich. Federman is a two-time Writers Guild Award nominee and also created the Annual Wayne Federman International Film Festival. For more, go to www.waynefederman.com and @Federman.

[Not in the Right Neighborhood]

HELEN GURLEY BROWN

editor in chief

English, John H. Francis Polytechnic High School,
Los Angeles, California

LET ME TELL YOU BRIEFLY about a teacher who seriously affected my life in my senior year of high school. Can I remember her name? Can I remember the name of the person who ran for vice president when Al Gore was elected president but lost the election because of the electoral college vote in Florida? No! Just let me say that this particular teacher encouraged me to write, though I was only sixteen years old. She perceived some modest talent. Of course, I didn't get a book written and published until twenty-six years later, but I know she helped (and I am feeling a little scruffy because I can't remember her name but I surely remember her gift). The name of the high school was John H. Francis Polytechnic High School in Los Angeles, California, way downtown, not in the right neighborhood.

HELEN GURLEY BROWN (1922–2012) was an author, publisher, and businesswoman. She was the editor in chief of *Cosmopolitan* magazine for thirty-two years.

[Ignited a Fire in Me]

JOHN GLENN
astronaut and senator

MR. DUITCH, physics,
MR. STEELE, civics,
New Concord High School, New Concord, Ohio

A TEACHER NAMED ELLIS DUITCH made basic physics and its practical applications interesting to me. He taught me how a radio worked and gave me some tips when I decided to build a crystal radio.

Harford Steele taught civics. Mr. Steele was a barrel-chested man who prided himself on the strength of his grip. He carried around a sponge ball that he would squeeze in one hand and then the other. Later, when he became the high-school principal and he gripped your shoulder to emphasize a point of discipline, you knew you'd been gripped. His civics course covered the fundamental institutions of the country, and he had a knack for making the whole thing come alive. He made history and government and politics into something really special. They were never remote, the way he taught them. You could see how individuals could exercise their beliefs and actually cause change and improvement. Citizenship in his terms was a dynamic practice. The idea that you really could make a difference stimulated me, partly because it reinforced what I had learned at home with Dad's participation on the school board. Mr. Steele's course ignited a fire in me that never did go out.

JOHN GLENN is a former astronaut who became the third person and first American to orbit the Earth. He began his career as a Marine Corps fighter pilot, before joining NASA's Mercury program, NASA's original astronaut group. He orbited the Earth aboard Friendship 7 in 1962. In 1998, at the age of seventy-seven, he became the oldest person to fly in space and the only person to fly on both the first and the most recent US space program (Mercury and Shuttle programs). He also served in the US Senate from 1974 to 1999 as a Democrat representing the state of Ohio.

[Unlimited Opportunities]

SHERRY LANSING
CEO

MATH TEACHER
University of Chicago High School, Chicago, Illinois

I GREW UP IN CHICAGO during the fifties. While a student at the University of Chicago High School, I took many math classes. On the first day of matrixes class my teacher talked to us about how difficult math had been for him when he was young. It had been his most challenging subject. In fact, he had failed math once before he came to love it. He wanted each one of his students to succeed and to get that same thrill from math that he did. He believed that each student should have as many chances as possible to succeed. He then explained that we would be allowed to take as long as we wanted during a test. If we didn't complete it during the class period that day, we could come by after class or before school the next morning to do so. He also said that if we still were uncertain about the subject matter and had not done well on the test we could take it again as many times as we liked, although the problems would be different. His philosophy was twofold. He believed that each student learns at a different pace. One student may get it on Monday, while the next might not for two more weeks. He also knew the anxiety that some students experience while taking a test. Knowing that I could take the test as many times as necessary, I learned that there were unlimited opportunities in math. He taught me the love of math that I had hoped for. This love of math is what pushed me to get my teaching certificate in math in college.

SHERRY LANSING is the former chairman and CEO of Paramount Pictures and the first woman to head a major studio. In 2001 *Ladies Home Journal* named her one of the thirty most powerful women in America. In 2005 she created the Sherry Lansing Foundation, which is dedicated to raising awareness and funds for cancer research and public education. In 2007 she received the Jean Hersholt Humanitarian Award at the Seventy-Ninth Annual Academy Awards, in recognition of her work in cancer research.

I DO NOT UNDERSTAND THE POWER of poetry to transfigure, but I remember the first time I experienced it. We had been studying composition in high school English, plowing through such necessary but rocky furrows as infinitives, genitives, and gerunds; the days were creaking by like turns of the torturer's rack. Then one morning Mrs. Hughes announced that we were changing course. We were going to study poetry. That is, she would read poems to us and we would listen, without commentary from her or questions from us. Inez Hughes could dissect a poem at ten paces with her eyes closed if she wished, but she insisted that poetry requires attention before it welcomes analysis.

So she read. Standing with her shoulders high and her back straight, and holding *The Oxford Book of English Verse* as far from her body as her arms would extend, she read. For the entire hour she read, until the bell rang and the spell was broken. She had a sonorous southern voice, as versatile as a pipe organ, which rose half an octave as she read. Between her native drawl and an exactness of diction acquired in elocution courses bask East, her sentences could flow like a languid stream or break, crisp and distinct, like twigs snapping under foot.

She liked Blake. She agreed with Wordsworth. And she was haunted by Thomas Gray. She often read Gray's elegy, and as she did, the poem took hold of me. Perhaps it was the rhythmic cadence: "The boast of heraldry, the pop of pow'r." Or the romantic imagery: "Full many a flower is born to blush unseen." Or the stark reality: "The paths of glory lead but to the grave." Most certainly my teacher's voice left as much of an imprint on me as the poet's verse. Several years later, during my first visit to England, I heard her voice in my head the moment I spied the gravestones in the churchyard at Stoke Poges that Gray immortalized. Reaching the vista that seemed so unchanged from the poem's evocation of it, I shivered slightly. I felt as if I had been there before and was even now experiencing the setting and the emotion as Gray experienced them two centuries earlier. Only twenty-two at the time, I felt sadness at the transience of all life. Thomas Gray may have felt nothing of the sort, of course; it may just have been the voice in my head, but such is poetry's power that the emotions awakened then are just as real to me now.

I was hooked that day in class, and Mrs. Hughes knew it. She began inviting me to her home, where she would read poems aloud as I devoured the cookies that she offered me. Occasionally she would hand me the book and suggest I read. But my adolescent voice sounded more like a rusty accordion than a pipe organ, and after one or two poems, she would gracefully retrieve the book, pass more cookies, and read on, until the light drained from the window, only crumbs were left on the plate, and it was time to go. We continued these sessions practically every week through the winter.

Fortunately, Inez Hughes was one of four consecutive teachers — from my final two years in high school through the first two years in college — who believed in reading aloud to their students. Either widows or spinsters, they were married to the English language. Selma Brotze loved Shelley, Keats, and Byron (although, being a good Presbyterian, she never divulged if she knew about the latter's raging promiscuity; for her, the poet was a cracked vessel, the poem its delicious and unspoiled nectar, and it was important not to confuse the two). Mary Tom Osborne preferred Thackeray, Tennyson, and Shakespeare. Eva Joy McGiffin plumbed Chaucer, Milton, and the Brownings, especially the Brownings.

BILL MOYERS began his journalism career at age sixteen as a cub reporter. Since then he has won too many awards to count, including more than thirty Emmys. In addition to broadcasting, Moyers was deputy director of the Peace Corps in the Kennedy administration and special assistant to President Johnson in 1963–1967. A trustee of the Rockefeller Foundation for twelve years, Moyers has served as president of the Florence and John Schumann Foundation.

[She Was Right]

ALETHEA BLACK
author

JUDY HESSION, AP adviser,
BARBARA NORTON, ninth-grade English,
Winchester, Massachusetts

MY PUBLIC HIGH SCHOOL in Winchester, Massachusetts, was filled with such extraordinary teachers that I chose to write one of my first short stories about a young woman who, twenty years later, looks up the English teacher she used to have a crush on. That story was entertaining to write, although I worried that if the real-life teacher ever read it, I'd have some explaining to do. But of course the real-life teacher was every bit as gracious and good-humored as his fictional counterpart, and the story ended well, both in life and on the page.

The handsome, young, guitar-playing crush wasn't the only teacher who left a lasting impression on me. My AP adviser, Judy Hession, had long, translucent fingernails and was rumored to be skilled at tarot readings. She had such fierce light in her eyes and such a passion for imaginary worlds that I had no trouble believing she might literally have access to other realms. And she did once prove to be psychic. After we read *Rosencrantz and Guildenstern Are Dead*, she had us go around the room and self-identify as either a "Rosencrantz" or a "Guildenstern" — which for our purposes meant either a follower or a leader. After I labeled myself a follower, a Rosencrantz, Miss Hession looked me dead in the eye and without hesitating told me I was a Rosencrantz disguised as a Guildenstern. I didn't understand what she meant at the time, but now that a few decades have passed, I can tell you: she was right.

And it was my ninth-grade English teacher who gave me one of the nicest compliments I've ever received. Barbara Norton had deformed fingers and toes that led some of the more imaginative freshmen to whisper that a childhood fire had left her disfigured. But I've come to believe she more likely had crippling rheumatoid arthritis, and was possibly in pain for much of the time we knew her. At any rate, she never spoke of her own health or comfort. One day she took me aside to tell me that a friend and fellow member of the English department faculty was depressed, and to cheer her up she'd read her a paragraph I'd written for our class assignment. I was so touched, I've never forgotten it. I've long since forgotten what I wrote, but I loved the idea that it might have lifted another human heart. I'm sure that same ambition is still part of what motivates me.

My own mother was a fourth-grade teacher at Brackett Elementary School in Arlington in the 1960s, and I've felt there was something special about the vocation for as long as I can remember. What amazes me most is the way a good teacher can make you feel unconditionally accepted and simultaneously spur you on to do better. Gerry Skinder, Judy Hession, and Barbara Norton burn most brightly in my memory, but I share in the debt we owe all teachers everywhere.

ALETHEA BLACK was born in Boston and graduated from Harvard in 1991. She was a three-time Moth StorySLAM champion, and her debut short story collection, *I Knew You'd Be Lovely* (2011), was chosen by the Barnes & Noble Discover Great New Writers program as well as by Oprah.com. Black lives in Los Angeles County with her miniature dachshund, Josie.

[Thanks, Mom]

DEAN KARNAZES
ultramarathon runner

MRS. KARNAZES
mom/teacher, Inglewood, California

I'VE ALWAYS HELD A SPECIAL PLACE IN MY HEART for teachers. Why? Because I was blessed with one of the greatest teachers in the world. She taught me about grammar and sentence structure, but more important, she taught me about the virtues of service and helping others. Her lessons on history and geography were valuable, though it was her education on the grace of living that left its deepest impression. She shared my success, and stuck by my side during my setbacks, which were often and many. Never did she pass judgment or convey doubt; quite the contrary, she trusted me more than I did myself. She could deliver a lesson plan with the best of them, yet she had the special gift of inspiring me to want to learn more, to care about the subject matter, to passionately embrace learning as a lifelong pursuit. Once, when faced with the difficult challenge of preparing my college entrance essays, she told me to think with my head but to write with my heart. I have since gone on to become a *New York Times*–bestselling author, writing two books and having numerous stories and essays printed in many noteworthy publications. I owe it all to her. Write with your heart, she told me. I will never forget those words. Thank you, Mrs. Karnazes. Thank you, Mom.

DEAN KARNAZES is a renowned ultramarathoner and a bestselling author. *Time* magazine ranked Karnazes as one of the "Top 100 Most Influential People in the World." Winner of the President's Council on Fitness, Sports & Nutrition Community Leadership Award, he is a monthly columnist for *Men's Health*.

[Thank You, Teacher]

[The Final Piece of the Puzzle]

LEE GREENWOOD
singer

FRED COOPER
music, Norte Del Rio High School, Sacramento, California

FRED COOPER was my high school music teacher. He understood my talent, my passion, and my need to succeed, and he gave me every opportunity to do so. My family moved twice before settling down in Sacramento, California, where I attended Norte Del Rio High for my junior and senior years. I was already proficient on the saxophone and clarinet, and I was eager for more. Mr. Cooper expanded my knowledge of instruments by allowing me to try anything I wanted to learn — which included the flute, trombone, trumpet, tympani, and snare drum — and encouraging me to be the drum major for the marching band in my senior year (quite a feat, since I was only 5'7" at the time; since then I've grown to be a whopping 5'8"). As I progressed through my senior year, Mr. Cooper prepared me for college by offering a new music class, music theory, to only three students. Learning how to write and arrange music would be the final piece of the puzzle I needed to leave home at seventeen and begin work in Nevada. I was offered a full ride to the College of the Pacific, but I opted to leave home and begin my life's work. I also played the vibraphone, banjo, and ukulele, and finally the piano, which was my mother's instrument. Singing came along as well, but it wasn't until I was twenty-two that it became the focus of my career.

Fred Cooper was a special teacher who understood his students and gave them choices that made sense to them. Often we overlook our children's desires and force our choices on them. Thanks go to Mr. Cooper and my grandparents for letting me make my own choices.

LEE GREENWOOD is a country music artist. He has released more than twenty major-label albums and has charted more than thirty-five singles on the *Billboard* country music charts, although he is best known for his top ten crossover single, "God Bless the USA."

[A Man of Passion]

DARRYL WIMBERLEY
author

MR. CUMBIE
English teacher and principal,
Lafayette County High School, Mayo, Florida

I WAS INTRODUCED TO SHAKESPEARE my senior year at a
rural and desperately underperforming consolidated school in
northwestern Florida. Lafayette County High School housed
all students, grades one through twelve, in an H-shaped bunker of concrete and jalousie windows built by the WPA sometime during the Depression. Our teacher for the forty or so
students who comprised the entire senior class came to us by
a fluke. Lafayette County's consolidated school was, and still
is, located about five miles from the Suwannee River in the
(very) small town of Mayo, Florida. There used to be two
schools in the county, not counting the segregated school in
Colored Town, which was in those years, and is still now in
some circles, easily discounted. The school other than Kerbo's
was a whites-only school in Day, Florida, an even smaller
burg just up the road from Mayo. DayTown's school burned
to the ground weeks before I entered the seventh grade. The
school's loss was terrible for its community to bear. The town

of Day died on the day its school was reduced to embers. One of the hardest-hit members of that community was the Reverend Herbert Cumbie. "Preacher" Cumbie, as he was locally known, was an ordained minister. Mr. Cumbie was also the principal at DayTown High School and its English teacher. He was a tall man with a high dome of a head and receding black hair. He had sloping shoulders and was a sloppy dresser. One of the first stories we heard about Mr. Cumbie was the account of how he had doused a blanket with water and rushed into Day's burning school to retrieve books from the fire-filled classrooms. He was reputed to be a man of passion. We all thought he must be just a little bit crazy. The citizens of Lafayette County could not afford to rebuild DayTown's school, even if they had been so inclined, and so all her students and most of the fallen school's excellent faculty were reshuffled without much ado to the fireproof and surviving school in Mayo where, in the seventh grade, the (white) populations of Day and Mayo were mixed. That was how Mr. Cumbie, and his children, came to us.

Mr. Cumbie was as close to a paterfamilias as could be imagined in a Protestant and conservative southern county. He guided us through *Silas Marner* and the Songs of Solomon with equal attention to detail. For a man so obviously hard on his own son and his family, Mr. Cumbie showed great restraint in disciplining his class, which is to say that he gave students their choice of punishments. He once let me take a paddling for Mike Tackett; I thought I was being cute. He wore my ass out. That combination of traits, by contemporary lights, would not seem a prepossessing choice for teaching literature of any kind, much less Shakespeare.

There were no texts for literature in our county school that bore any hint of the Bard or his works. Nothing of Steinbeck, either, or Ray Bradbury, or Faulkner, a curious lapse for a school full of students sweating in un-air-conditioned rooms in a land that would be familiar to the Snopeses, or any similar family. There was nothing on the shelves of our classroom to offend, but nothing to challenge, either. Nothing, at any rate, that raised to any serious level questions involving the triumvirate of God, guns, and authority. But Mr. Cumbie had a rare gift for a man otherwise ruled by absolutes, which is to say that he was not afraid to challenge his own beliefs. At his own expense, our teacher purchased used paperbacks of three or four of Shakespeare's tragedies. Herbert Cumbie was willing to risk whatever subversion might occur with readings of *Macbeth* or *Julius Caesar* or *Othello* because he could not imagine young people claiming any degree of education who were not willing to wrestle with those works, accept their hard assessments of the human condition, and pursue the questions raised. Not that the Reverend Cumbie, with his hard-shell Baptist hermeneutics, was unwilling to edit the Bard's unholy text: "To be or not to be" is not the whole question, Mr. Cumbie admonished us constantly. "The question is whether we are to be, or not to be, good for something."

Mr. Cumbie eventually located nearer to Mayo and his new classroom. He pastored Airline Baptist Church, barely two miles from my homestead, and with his own hands built a house, which still stands. He was a gunner on a destroyer in World War II. He drove a Comet, last I remember, driving that small car as though he had a whip in hand, as if there were not time enough in the world to save every soul, educate every child, buck every bigoted idea or attitude that he was, constitutionally, unable to resist opposing.

He was a mad shepherd. Every girl and boy in Lafayette County's all-white school was important to this man's soul-seeking ministry. It was impossible to emerge from Preacher

Cumbie's classroom unchanged or untouched. Within a few years boys would be changed to men in Southeast Asia. Mr. Cumbie, a navy veteran himself from the Second World War, was never a cheerleader for that expedition. He spoke from the pulpit candidly, and more obliquely in the classroom, stating that *dulce et decorum est pro patria mori*. He was a hard father, I am sure, an impassioned educator, and a preacher.

Mr. Cumbie died, with his wife, driving too fast on a return trip from some revival in Alabama. His orphaned children were taken in by a family in the area. His son would stand beside me at our high school graduation. A fire brought us Mr. Cumbie. A fire would take him away, but not so far that his own burning heat cannot still be felt.

DARRYL WIMBERLEY was born in St. Augustine, Florida. His works include *A Rock and a Hard Place*, *Dead Man's Bay*, *Strawman's Hammock*, *Pepperfish Keys*, *A Tinker's Damn*, and *The King of Colored Town*, which was awarded the Willie Morris Prize for Southern Fiction in 2008. Wimberley writes full-time in Austin, Texas. He is married and has two children.

You'll Never Amount to a Hill of Beans

KEITH JACKSON

sportscaster

MS. MARY BAXTER
Carrollton, Georgia

GRADUATING FROM A LITTLE COUNTRY HIGH SCHOOL in West Georgia in 1946, I was determined to join the US Marines as quickly as possible. Everyone in my family had been marines, going back to the twenties, and though the big war was over I wanted to go. Leaving a graduating class of twenty-eight, off I went. I fibbed a little, about four months' worth, and was accepted. I guess they were happy to find some eager young pups after the long struggle of World War II. On my departure one of my favorite teachers, Ms. Mary Baxter, hammered me and my decision and left me with these cutting words, "If you go with the marines you will never amount to a hill of beans and you'll probably get killed." That was a southern lady talking, mind you! Those words still ring in my ears more than six decades later, especially when I face a challenging moment. And there have been many of those in my life; I have traveled across thirty-three countries, and I don't really know how many millions of miles. It doesn't matter! What mattered was the challenge that teacher threw at me from the steps of that old red brick schoolhouse when I was sixteen and thought I was bulletproof. The teacher almost never knows which words will have the most meaning for those who have gone...but bless 'em for keeping on.

If I ever chance to see Miss Mary again, I will be happy to tell her that in my fifty-four years of professional life I had two jobs and one great and glorious wife and three children. Which clearly proves I don't know a damned thing about show business.

KEITH JACKSON is a former sportscaster known for his long career with ABC Sports television, his coverage of college football, his deep voice, and his style of folksy, down-to-earth commentary, coining the lines, "Whoa, Nellie!" and "Fum-BLE!"

[Unquestioned Authority]

ROBERT PINSKY
poet

MR. ANGUS MACWITHEY
woodshop and mechanical drawing,
Long Branch High School, Long Branch, New Jersey

WITH UNQUESTIONED AUTHORITY Mr. Angus MacWithey taught woodshop and mechanical drawing to unruly adolescent boys, including the Bad Class, as our group was called. He never raised his voice or made a threat. However, he wielded a lethal, pale blue stare of disapproval, supported by a samurai carriage of his body.

He led us would-be thugs into the first intellectual discussion I can remember. How do you determine the front of an object, he asked?

Um, if it moved, the side that would go first? (Then which side of a factory would that be?) The largest side? (Then which side of a cube would that be?) The part where something comes in or out? (So the front of a toilet is from below, or above? Or is the front of your car where the doors are? Or the trunk?) We reasoned and theorized for a session of some length. Juvenile-delinquent philosophers, Aristotelian hoodlums. So Mr. MacWithey taught us the nature of definition.

He also taught analogical thinking. A Rip saw can be distinguished from a Crosscut because the Rip teeth have the shape made by the upright and leg of the letter R.

I brought him my drawing, the dimension lines and drawing lines executed with distinguishing degrees of pressure, laboriously, as he told us to do. Something's missing, he said. What, Mr. Mac? Gently he tapped my head, then his. I had forgotten the arrowheads on the dimension lines.

An arrowhead, he taught us, is not a graceless V plunked at the tip of a dimension line like two ribs of a broken umbrella teetering on its handle. The twin barbs of an arrowhead should curve gracefully away from the dimension line's tip, like water dividing away from the point of a boat's prow. So he taught the significance of formal beauty, and its traditions, as well.

Once he ordered me to tell the class my semester grade: A. He commended me to the other little brutes: someone with not much talent who had worked hard. (In English, social studies, mathematics, I was getting Ds and Cs, and the occasional F.) He taught me to value work, and to understand that I was capable of work. He respected his material and he respected us: on principle and because that was his work.

(The front of an object is the view that gives the most information about it.)

ROBERT PINSKY's most recent books are his *Selected Poems* (2011) and *Singing School* (2014), an anthology-cum-manifesto. Circumstantial Productions has released *House Hour*, his second PoemJazz CD with Grammy-winning pianist Laurence Hobgood.

[To Be Inspired, to Inspire]

INDIRA CESARINE
photographer

JOHN FAULKNER
photography, Choate Rosemary Hall, Wallingford, Connecticut

EDUCATION SHAPES YOUR LIFE in ways unforeseen. As a student one is rarely aware of the influence certain teachers may have on you, or how later in life you are shaped by their support.

I consider myself fortunate in my educational choices. At the age of thirteen, I made a rather unusual decision for a girl who grew up in Des Moines, Iowa. It was 1984, and with the influence of popular books like *The Preppy Handbook* raging throughout America, I decided that I wanted to go to an East Coast boarding school. In Des Moines the only students "sent away" to boarding school were being punished for bad behavior rather than being awarded for academic excellence. I saw the opportunity as a way to find my own expression and explore my identity in an environment that would nurture my individuality rather than suppress it. With top PSAT scores and straight As in hand, I applied to several schools. My older sister accompanied me to my interviews, and the school that stood out the most was Choate Rosemary Hall. The impressive school campus, the strong support of the arts, and the ethnic diversity of the students inspired me.

Choate Rosemary Hall is famous for its legendary alumni, including John F. Kennedy, Paul Mellon, Michael Douglas, Glenn Close, Ivana Trump, and the sons and daughters of some of the world's top international leaders. I expected to be intimidated by the school and the students, but I found the experience extremely rewarding. Going to class every day in buildings built by architects such as the celebrated I. M. Pei (renowned for the pyramid at the Louvre) further inspired creative thought and made going to classes something to look forward to.

During the summer of 1986 I attended the Parsons School of Design "Summer Program for High School Students" in Manhattan for photography and discovered what would become a lifelong passion. I was immediately absorbed by the magic of photography. I found that the process of developing film and printing photos allowed me to express myself in a way that I never could before. The spontaneous moments captured by still photography opened up a whole new world.

To this day I remember one teacher whom I will always recognize as being truly supportive of my creativity, and that was John Faulkner, the head of the photography department at Choate Rosemary Hall. After seeing the work I created at Parsons, and in one of his classes, he created an independent study program for me, with access to a private darkroom on campus as well as a photographic studio space at the Paul Mellon Art Center (built from the $100,000,000 Endowment for the Arts made to Choate by the Mellon Family). John Faulkner encouraged my independence, recognizing that I worked better on my own than in a classroom environment, since I was so passionate about my work. In the program he created for me I worked on my own time and reported to him once a week to show him my photos. He encouraged advanced darkroom and lighting techniques as well as medium format work. Each term I presented an exhibit of my work, with the subjects varying from portraiture and nudes to documentary-style images of New York nightlife.

Looking back at my experience working with John Faulkner makes me appreciate the freedom he afforded me by encouraging my independent study and allowing my access to facilities to hone my craft. I was lucky enough to be a student at Choate Rosemary Hall, and even more fortunate to have the encouragement of a teacher who recognized my need for expression and independence.

INDIRA CESARINE had her first solo exhibition at the age of sixteen at the Paul Mellon Arts Center. She is a multimedia artist who works with photography, video, painting, printmaking, and sculpture. Her work has been exhibited internationally at many art galleries, museums, and festivals, including the Metropolitan Museum of Art, the Getty Images Gallery, the San Diego Museum of Contemporary Art, the French Embassy Cultural Center, Art Basel Miami, the Cannes Film Festival, and the International Festival Photo Mode. In 2014 her public art sculpture *The Egg of Light* was exhibited at Rockefeller Center. In 2009 she launched a publication, *The Untitled Magazine*, of which she is editor in chief. Cesarine has been featured internationally on TV shows and networks and lives in Tribeca, New York.

[The Death-Defying Mr. G]

WILLIAM LASHNER
author

MR. GIORDANO
honors English, Abington Senior High School, Abington, Pennsylvania

I MET GREGOR in Mr. Giordano's tenth-grade English class. Gregor was older than the rest of us, was already working to support his family, and carried a melancholy that covered him like a shroud. Yet strangely I found we had much in common. We both were suffering a near-paralyzing alienation. We both were anxious about our futures. And Gregor had awoken one morning to find himself transformed into an insect, which meant we had about an equal chance of getting a date on a Saturday night.

Many years later, Gregor was one of the obvious inspirations for a pseudonymous novel I wrote called *Kockroach*, the story of a cockroach inhabiting a fleabag Times Square hotel who wakes one night to find himself transformed into a man. Other inspirations included an Edward Hopper painting, a Louis Armstrong song, a former girlfriend named Gwen, and the kitchen of my East Village apartment. But beyond all those, there was Mr. Giordano himself, the amazing Mr. G.

Mr. Giordano also introduced us to Gregor's pal Joseph K., one of those kids who always got called down to the principal's office for no reason. And Meursault, who sat in the last row of class smoking cigarettes and making time with Marie while not caring about anyone or anything, certainly not his mother's funeral. And Roquentin, who had severe gastrointestinal issues. And Job, such a complainer I could barely stand to be in the room with him. And then that big Greek kid who hung out in the weight room day and night, day and night.

You enter a tenth-grade English class expecting to be spoon-fed huge chunks of turgid prose, to read a socially aware novel or two, to maybe tackle a bit of Shakespeare. You don't go into tenth-grade English class expecting to get gobsmacked with unsettling questions about the meaning of life. But there was Mr. G, throwing Kafka and Camus at us with malicious glee.

It's easy enough to conduct a brilliant class by teaching amazing authors, but it was the clarity with which Mr. Giordano taught the ideas in the books that made all the difference. Behind the characters and stories lay a whole universe of existential thought that Mr. G, through the precision of his understanding and the depth of his passion, brought to life for us. We entered that class the callowest of youths; we left it still remarkably, even proudly, callow but with an arrow in our quivers for making some sense of our universe and our lives. It wasn't the only arrow; there would be many others: God, and politics, and love, and family, and the great triumvirate of sex and drugs and rock and roll. But whenever, even decades later, those of us who had the great good fortune to be part of that class pondered our fates, Mr. G was always part of the discussion.

To say that Mr. Giordano was the best teacher I ever had

doesn't do his influence on me justice. It would be more accurate to say that he, more than anyone, was responsible for my becoming a writer. It wasn't that he recognized the worthiness of my prose and encouraged my efforts, because I was an indifferent student, and my high school writing efforts were unfocused and limp. It was more that you left Mr. Giordano's class with an intuitive understanding of the absolute centrality of art. Literature spoke to the noblest yearnings and deepest doubts; literature was the field where the questions were always more vital than the answers. After a year with Mr. G, where else would I want to play?

I dedicated *Kockroach* to Mr. Giordano, and when I gave him an inscribed copy of the novel I told him he should consider it my tenth-grade honors thesis. In a way, I had crammed a little bit of him onto every page. We had dinner with some of my former classmates to celebrate the publication, and all those years later he was just as captivating, his drive to wrest meaning from an indifferent universe just as furious. Mr. G was finished with teaching by then and had retired to a lovely house in Doylestown. After dinner he invited us to his home, and we couldn't help but notice a sculpture of the Buddha in his fireplace.

"So, Mr. G," said one of us, "have you found some inner peace through meditation and Eastern teachings?"

His head turned suddenly, as if he had been insulted. "What makes you think that?"

"The Buddha in your fireplace."

"It's decorative," he said, a bitter snap in his voice that made it perfectly clear that no, he had not found inner peace, had no intention of finding inner peace, thank you very much. As Camus wrote in an essay Mr. Giordano assigned to us when we were sixteen, "There is no fate that cannot be surmounted by scorn." Thirty-five years had passed, and Mr. G's scorn was undiminished. He was still the teacher.

Mr. Giordano later called and said he liked my novel very much, and I appreciated his kind words, even knowing he was too much of a gentleman to have said anything else. But I can honestly say I wasn't sitting on tenterhooks waiting for his response. Among the things he taught us was that the opinions of others meant little, that the battle to forge a life and make a contribution is ours alone to wage.

None of us will ever forget the sight of Mr. G in a toga, down on one knee, pushing a mythical rock up a mythical hill and reciting Camus's immortal lines: "The struggle itself toward the heights is enough to fill a man's heart. One must imagine Sisyphus happy." For a teacher, the struggle to enlighten a pack of unruly teens must have seemed just as Sisyphean. I don't know if we left Mr. Giordano happy or herniated, but he left us soaring.

WILLIAM LASHNER is the *New York Times*–bestselling author of *Guaranteed Heroes*; *The Barkeep*, a Zen-infused standalone and Digital Book World #1 Bestseller; and *The Accounting*, as well as eight novels featuring Victor Carl, whom *Booklist* called one of the mystery novel's "most compelling, most morally ambiguous characters." A graduate of the Iowa Writers' Workshop and the New York University School of Law, Lashner was a prosecutor with the Department of Justice in Washington, DC, before quitting the law to write full-time.

[All Things Pass]

ANTHONY BOZZA
author

MR. BROGAN
English, Friends Academy, Locust Valley, Long Island, New York

THREE WORDS ON A CHALKBOARD. One man, standing before them, in his uniform: a simple tweed jacket, square tortoiseshell glasses, a buttoned-down broadcloth shirt and silk bow tie, and well-worn brown leather shoes. It wasn't the first day of class and it wasn't my first class with him, but that day he taught me more than any other teacher has taught me before or since. Those three words disseminated the wisdom he'd found in literature and in life more effectively than a library full of books could ever do. I'll forever be in awe of and in debt to Mr. Frank Brogan for offering us the key to life as he saw it, so simply, so precisely, and so humbly. The best lessons are never shouted. His have saved me more times than he'll ever know.

Mr. Brogan was of average size, but his presence loomed large. He'd been a marine in World War II and stormed the beach at Normandy. He did not tolerate any kind of misbehavior in his classroom. Those who made the mistake of causing a ruckus on his watch discovered that a keen mind and an observational eye are devastating weapons because Mr. Brogan made fools of class clowns and silenced chatterboxes with eloquent grace. He never brandished his power directly; he disarmed by dissection. He understood human nature, comprehending great works of literature as easily as he did the mind-set of his students. He wed the two with seamless aplomb. He strove to teach us that no matter how different they may be, all human stories share commonalities. At the end and in the beginning, after all, we are one and the same.

Mr. Brogan was feared more than he was adored. Those who understood what he was really teaching us revered him like no other. He lived as he taught: thoughtfully, seriously, and consistently. His wife worked in my school, and on the chance occasion that she passed his classroom during the day, Mr. Brogan's face warmed with a smile befitting a love-struck teen. To see him giddy at the sight of her after so many years of living and working beside each other was inspiring to me.

One day during my senior year, Mr. Brogan asked me to stay after class. There was no obvious reason: my grades were high, I participated regularly, and I never misbehaved (in his class, at least). But he saw what I'd been hiding: my parents' marriage was disintegrating. As an only child it was hard to bear. After the other students had left, he asked me quite directly how life was at home. He had a gaze like no one else's I've ever met: his blue-gray eyes were as dense as polar ice yet twinkled from within with the warmth of wisdom. For the next few minutes I enjoyed the freedom of true honesty. I hadn't told anyone about the fissure in my nuclear family and had no intention of doing so. Mr. Brogan, a teacher who'd taught me English for two years and observed me only within the confines of his class, had seen what I'd tried so hard to hide and cared enough to draw me out.

Mr. Brogan didn't offer easy solace, empathy, or coffee-table psychology; he shared the wisdom that had served him well through trials and tribulations more drastic than any I'd ever known. The best way to weather life's storms, he said, was to bury yourself in the right book.

I've followed my share of paths to freedom since then, and that piece of advice has done me more good than the hours, dollars, and mental exertion I've spent elsewhere. The right book will open your eyes by being your mirror. With the right book in hand you will never be alone. When I finished college, the same year my parents finally divorced, I was entirely at sea, just another lost soul with a bachelor's degree. I sought structure and thought I'd find it in law school. It seemed a likely place to land. The summer before I made that decision, I sought out Mr. Brogan, who had retired from teaching.

He'd softened a bit since leaving the classroom, but his keen eyes had lost none of their luster. Sitting on his porch, he fixed those eyes on me and once again became my teacher. He told me to read *One L* by Scott Turow. It's a memoir of the bestselling legal thriller author's first year as a student at Harvard Law School. "It doesn't matter whether you like his fiction writing, Tony," Mr. Brogan said. "All you need to know about the experience of law school is in there. He captures it completely. Read it before you make any decisions. You'll know if law is right for you far before you reach the end."

Law wasn't for me, but it very well could have become my life. For that I owe Mr. Brogan everything. He never told me what to be or do; he gave me the tools to learn who I am on my own. At that point in my life, I asked him a simple question and he gave me a simple answer. He reminded me of what he'd taught us all along. As important and critical as human folly might seem at the time, all things pass. We can build structures against what we see as chaos, but time will always win. In this life we must be true to ourselves because, in time, all things pass.

ANTHONY BOZZA is a former *Rolling Stone* staff writer and the author of four *New York Times* bestsellers. He grew up on Long Island and attended Friends Academy, one of several Quaker schools on the East Coast.

ELLIE KRIEGER

dietitian and author

MR. YOHALEM

biology, New York, New York

NEVER UNDERESTIMATE SMALL THINGS. Sometimes they are what affect us most deeply and lastingly. My high school biology teacher didn't turn my life around or rescue me from horrible circumstances or become my closest friend. He simply took the time to listen one afternoon, and it stuck with me the rest of my life.

At my enormous, bustling New York City public high school, one-on-one conversations with teachers were usually rushed and to the point, sentences plucked from the din in the hallways. I always felt more intimidated by my teachers than connected with them. Not so with Mr. Yohalem, who had a gentle kindness, playful approachability, and thoughtful wisdom about him. It was that demeanor and a tremendous respect for him that led me to turn to him for advice one afternoon.

As a senior I faced a critical decision about what college to attend, and I was confused about what would be best for me. When I approached Mr. Yohalem with my problem, he did the most amazing thing. He closed the door, sat down with me, and really listened! He carefully contemplated my options, explored my concerns, and offered me his wise suggestions. His generosity with his time was probably so ordinary for him that he had no idea he was affecting me so meaningfully. But he made me feel valued, as if my future were something important and precious, and it stuck with me forever.

So teachers, know this: each and every day you do small things that profoundly affect your students. Listening, believing, being a role model, and taking the time to understand a child are seemingly ordinary acts that are truly extraordinary.

ELLIE KRIEGER is a *New York Times*–bestselling author. She helps people of all ages achieve balance in food, health, and life and have joy right at their fingertips. She is a registered dietitian and host of a hit show, *Healthy Appetite*, on Food Network.

┌─────────────────────────────────────┐

[A World of Possibility]

NICOLA KRAUS
author

MR. EUGENE GARDINO
AP physics, New York, New York

└─────────────────────────────────────┘

ONE WOULD PROBABLY EXPECT that, as a professional writer, I would want to use this opportunity to extol one of the many English teachers who encouraged my love of storytelling. And I am thankful for every one of them, but the teacher who changed my life taught AP physics.

Now, as with most creative types, science was not a subject in which my verbosity helped me or endeared me to any of my teachers. I had essentially squeaked by, thinking of myself as an artist with no aptitude for math or science. But in eleventh grade, forced to make the Solomonic decision between chemistry and physics, I chose physics. I'm still not sure why.

Mr. Eugene Gardino was our teacher, and he brought to the class not only a crackling sense of humor and a clear way of explaining things that made even subatomic particles comprehensible to a sixteen-year-old but a passion for the poetry of physics. Under his guidance I became obsessed with this system that suddenly revealed the underpinnings of our world, from the vector of a gunshot to why the siren of an ambulance sounds at a higher pitch approaching you than receding (the Doppler effect).

Two favorite memories inspire me to quote Mr. Gardino often. The first is of him explaining to us that every step we take on the planet moves it backward, as it would if we were a clown walking on a rubber ball. But on the opposite side of the world someone is walking toward us, and all our footsteps cancel each other out. Then someone asked, "But Mr. Gardino, what would happen if everyone lined up and took a step together?" He paused a brief moment, considering how to answer. "Well, then we could *really* get this sucker to roll." I still like to think of the Earth that way, like a big rubber ball that could be under our control if only all of humanity could just agree on an action.

My second memory is from later in the year, when we had moved on to more advanced particle physics, and he was relating to us the facts of a famous experiment that I still read about in the *Times'* Science section from time to time. A photon was fired through a surface with two slits into a metal wall that would record its position. The slits were opened and closed at random. In theory the proton should have made it through, on average, only half the time. *But the proton always made it through*. Somehow it course-corrected, as if it had eyes. Mr. Gardino was staring out at thirty gobsmacked girls who couldn't have been more on the edge of our seats if he'd been telling a ghost story. "So, girls, the question is..." he paused dramatically. "How does the photon know?" It is a question that still baffles physicists today.

The love of physics he engendered in me changed the way I thought about myself and how my brain worked. I never imagined that in my twenties I would eagerly watch a Brian

Greene special on *Nova*. Or integrate concepts of string theory into my yoga practice.

My English teachers nurtured my strengths, but Mr. Gardino exposed me to a world of possibility, both externally and internally, that I had never imagined.

NICOLA KRAUS is the coauthor of the *New York Times* bestsellers *The Nanny Diaries*, *Nanny Returns*, *Citizen Girl*, *Dedication*, and *The Real Real*. In 2007 *The Nanny Diaries* was released as a motion picture starring Scarlett Johansson.

He Taught Me
More Important Life Skills

BRIAN CROSBY

author and teacher

MR. SAGE

English, John Burroughs High School, Burbank, California

AT AGE FIFTEEN, in 1974, my body was attacked by psoriasis, from my scalp down to my eyelids and all around my joints, down to my feet. I was miserable. It was the worst time of my life, even more than the previous year, when my dad died, for while I was sad about my father's passing, his yearlong battle with lung cancer affected me emotionally but not physically, whereas psoriasis was interfering with my day-to-day existence.

I didn't want people to know about my psoriasis, especially my classmates and teachers. Yet somehow one of my teachers, knowing that I'd be absent for a month, hospitalized at UCLA (about fifteen miles from home), made an effort to locate me and visit me a couple of times, always bringing classic literature like *Great Expectations* with him as gifts.

John Sage, or Mr. Sage (I never could call him by his first name, even years later), was my advanced tenth-grade English teacher at John Burroughs High School in Burbank. He was always immaculately dressed in a suit, with shiny black dress shoes. He'd remove his suit jacket only when the temperature reached triple digits (the school wasn't air-conditioned then). To this day, I emulate his professional attire at the school where I teach.

Yes, he taught me Shakespeare's *Julius Caesar*, but more important, he taught me life skills.

Mr. Sage introduced me to fine dining, treating me at the famed Hollywood restaurant the Brown Derby. I learned that dining was different from eating, and that dressing up to go out to eat and to the theater was one of life's splendid pleasures.

I remember we went across the street from the Brown Derby to the historic Huntington Hartford Theatre to see Eugene O'Neill's *The Iceman Cometh*, with famed stage and screen actor Jason Robards reprising his career-making role as Hickey, which he originally played in 1956. (I was amazed at the amount of energy he needed to do a nearly five-hour long play, to memorize all those lines — thirty years later.)

Once he retired near the Pacific Ocean in San Clemente, Mr. Sage would invite me down for gourmet dinners. I fondly remember sitting at the table in his kitchen, talking to him about everything in my life as he patiently listened and cooked at the same time.

He taught me how to make mixed drinks (I was over twenty-one by then), including his favorite, the Manhattan. That was the only help in the kitchen he would allow. As he cooked and we talked, I would munch on mixed nuts, which he had set on the table and which went so well with my drink.

When dinner was ready (at least two hours later), he served me in his formal dining room. Part of this ritual included educating me on after-dinner liqueurs as a sophisticated way to finish a meal. When Mr. Sage was in good spirits, he would go to the piano and play and sing. I especially recall him serenading me with "September Song."

On many of my visits, I would bring a friend, or he would have a friend over. I loved these evenings of good food and good conversation.

As Mr. Sage got older, his health declined. Soon he was no longer able to cook elaborate meals, so I would pick up food from a restaurant and we'd eat it in his dining room.

When he could no longer live alone, he invited me to drive down one last time to take any books from his extensive classic literature collection that I liked. That was not a fun visit. It was like an estate sale but with the owner still living.

Soon he would be transported from an assisted living facility to a hospital to a nursing home. I visited him at each place. Each time he seemed frailer. Each visit would be shorter than the previous one.

My final visit to him was when I had sold my first book. I was excited to share this with him because he was such an inspiration to me as a teacher.

Soon thereafter, I received a phone call informing me that he had died. It's a shame he didn't live long enough to see my published book, for the dedication was to him, "to all hard-working teachers who deserve better, most especially my mentor, John Sage."

BRIAN CROSBY is a National Board Certified high school English teacher in the Los Angeles area and the author of *Smart Kids, Bad Schools: 38 Ways to Save America's Future* and *The $100,000 Teacher: A Teacher's Solution to America's Declining Public School System*, columnist of "The Whiteboard Jungle" for the *Los Angeles Times* community newspapers, and a blogger on his websites, www.briancrosby.org and www.crosby chronicles.org. Crosby has appeared numerous times on national TV and radio discussing educational issues.

[Don't Know Anyone Like Him]

JOE WILKINS
author

MR. WHEARTY
English, Melstone High School, Melstone, Montana

IF SOME BOYS START MESSING AROUND, he doesn't look the other way or shake his finger — he throws them up against the wall. And not just the bad ones. He'll take the good boys who are being bad and throw them up against the wall too. He'll throw just about any boy up against the wall and then hold him there by the armpits or with bunched fistfuls of winter coat, the boy's sneakered feet swinging just above the blacktop, and Mr. Whearty — his dark beard wild about his face; his black, thick-rimmed glasses framing his dark eyes; and that smell of him, of earth and burnt coffee and prairie weeds, of someone who lives half the year in a tepee down on the Musselshell River and doesn't use deodorant and doesn't care — he'll say, "Tell me what you did, and why it was wrong, and then you can go."

The folks around town shake their heads and say that Mr. Whearty is a hippie, a tree hugger, a radical. But my mother — who doesn't wear makeup, who, even though our turntable is broken and we don't have the money to fix it, every now and again gets out her old Joan Baez and Gordon Lightfoot records and runs her hands across those worn, dusty covers — tells me that folks around here only call Mr. Whearty those names because they don't know what else to call him, don't know anyone like him.

I think maybe my mother's right. Sure, Mr. Whearty writes letter after letter to the president. Sure, he refuses to watch TV. But all summer he cuts and stacks cords of pine wood outside his tepee, and he stays as warm as the rest of us all winter. And you should see him teach. There's no I'm-okay-you're-okay nonsense. He simply will not abide students putting their heads down on their desks during algebra. He makes us turn in our homework first thing every morning. He has us analyze stories and poems, has us deliver, in front of the whole class, the speeches of Abraham Lincoln and Chief Joseph and Martin Luther King Jr. And he especially will not allow for tardiness, bullying, or dishonesty.

This is all news to us. We have only just finished with dioramas and clay models as major educational undertakings, but Mr. Whearty doesn't care. He has a chart and makes us read real books, lots of them. He has us perform *Macbeth* for the whole school up on the main stage. When Halloween comes around, he dresses up like a pancreas. He just doesn't care. Or maybe it's that he does care. Anyway, Mr. Whearty plans a Squid Fest, complete with squid dissection, squid feast, and interpretive squid dance. There is a squid-trivia competition too, which I win, which makes me the Squid King. I am proud to be the Squid King. And Mr. Whearty is proud of me — but not too proud. He still makes me work. He pushes me from bright-covered fantasy paperbacks to Tolkien and Le Guin, hands me *A Tree Grows in Brooklyn* and *A River Runs Through*

It. I read them all, I read and read and like Mr. Whearty do not apologize for it. In fact, I begin to glory in it. I get as smart and weird as I want, and I don't care what the other kids think.

Today, though, I have lost my book. I was reading Steinbeck, *Of Mice and Men.* I liked it. I didn't mean to lose it. I don't know what's happened to it. And because my face goes bright and hot even at the thought of doing something wrong, I have been for most of the morning trying to figure out how to tell Mr. Whearty the truth and still stay out of trouble. Maybe, I finally decide, it's a matter of presentation. So when we sit down for our one-on-one reading session, I fold my hands in my lap and say, clearly, as if there is no other way to put it, "My book was lost."

"No," Mr. Whearty says, loudly.

I feel like I might fall out of my chair. I start to sputter.

"You lost it," he says, cutting me off. "It was not just lost, as if you are not responsible, as if it had the power of locomotion. It is a book. It is not animate. It did not get up and go hide from you. No. You are responsible. You lost it. Tell me that you lost it."

I blink back tears, mumble, "I lost it."

"Yes, you did. But we'll find you another copy." He rises to leave but looks down at me again. "And don't use the passive voice. It's sloppy. It confuses subject and object, and then we no longer understand action. You know better than that. Don't do it."

He has never said anything like this to me before. I mean, I was the Squid King. As Mr. Whearty walks away, I stare, shamed, at my shoes. And at the end of the term, when the school board sort of encourages Mr. Whearty to leave, and he does leave, I pretend I'm as happy as all those boys he threw up against the wall.

Joe Wilkins is the author of a memoir, *The Mountain and the Fathers*, and the poetry collections *Notes from the Journey Westward* and *Killing the Murnion Dogs*. A Pushcart Prize winner and National Magazine Award finalist, he lives with his family in western Oregon and teaches writing at Linfield College.

[Ça Va]

RACHEL TOOR
author

HARRY WESTON
French, Courtland Jr./Sr. High School, Courtland, New York

HE WAS, PERHAPS, THE LEAST LIKELY TEACHER to allow us to call him by his first name. It's possible older students passed along the practice the way they handed down textbooks, with signs of use and traces of erasure. Or maybe he invited the familiarity. I never asked or wondered about it.

Unlike the other teachers, Harry dressed impeccably, and with a certain tweedy flair. I want to remember him wearing an ascot, but that seems a tick too far. Did a splash of handkerchief color peek from his pocket? Did he sport a gold bracelet? Harry's air of sophistication trailed him like cologne, at odds with our town's agricultural vibe. And he had a gentleness I was unaccustomed to in a man. In an upstate New York town known for apples and a college that produced jocks, Harry Weston stood out.

I started taking French in ninth grade, around the same time my stacks of Agatha Christie paperbacks had reached wobbly heights. I thought of Harry as somehow like Hercule

Poirot. Perhaps it was the mustache, though Harry's was neatly trimmed. Perhaps it was a certain finicky composure. Perhaps it was because we harbored unasked questions about his private life. In the late 1970s a refined, unmarried, middle-aged man was suspect.

It's improbable to me now that a teacher, so precise in his diction, so meticulous in his bearing, ran such a loud and boisterous classroom, and let loose in me an obstreperous persona I rarely showed in public. In my memory I sit on, rather than behind, a desk, conjugating *faire* in the pluperfect and trying to pronounce *heureuse*. I don't remember other teachers from high school; I don't remember learning anything worth retaining. Mostly I kept my head down, breezed through the work, and then went home to read. Bored and tortured, I wrote poems and itched to leave a place I viewed as provincial and which, though I'd spent nearly all my life there, never felt like home.

My father, an English professor, taught by intimidation. He condescended to his students in class and complained about them at home. He made dinner reservations, and announced himself to bank tellers using the honorific "Dr." He dressed like a janitor, in matching blue work pants and shirt with a jangle of keys on his belt that announced his arrival long before he walked into a room. He blasted classical music out of a Bang & Olufsen stereo my mother said we couldn't afford, asked the dog to sit *en français*, and swore *ay caramba!* and *merde alors!* when he fixed electronics.

If I had spoken to my father the way I did to my French teacher, had challenged, defied, and teased him the way I did Harry, my father would have raised his hand in threat and I would have abased myself and slunk away. His temper was explosive and unpredictable. For my father, nothing was ever good enough; he made me feel that I would never be good enough. I did well in school, behaved outside of it, and turned his perceived disappointment in on myself. I learned to use self-hatred to fuel achievement.

Harry never got angry, even when I contradicted him in class, even when I tried to provoke him. I'd heard a native French speaker claim that Americans are never able to get French pronunciation right. I shared this with Harry and he responded with a sad smile, "I don't believe that to be true."

Did Harry know that I needed a place to be a little bit wild? I'm sure I never discussed my home life with him, never told him how my father's love felt contingent, dependent on my performance. All these years later I want to believe that Harry saw me not just for who I was at the time — an angry, hurt, frustrated teen who waxed rude and disrespectful — but for who I could become. In the words of that '70s anthem, I felt free to be me, even if that wasn't always a good thing.

Like my father's, Harry's language was peppered with allusions to the many books he'd imbibed. When a red-cheeked boy too often teased for being smart decided to transfer out of French class, Harry signed his name giving approval and wrote on the form, *Sic transit gloria mundi*. Did the women in the office have any idea what that meant? Did the boy? I didn't, but Harry translated it, let me in on the joke. He made me feel smart, an unseasoned sensation.

Even after my guidance counselor told me I had no hope of getting into my first-choice college, after she'd said no one from our high school had ever been admitted, I asked Harry for a letter of recommendation. I worried I may have gone too far with him, that I had been too abrasive in class, too familiar. I don't know what he said about me in that letter. Don't know if, when I got in, he was proud.

My father rarely said he was proud of me, but he made me get a college decal for the back windshield of our car. In what felt like a small act of rebellion I picked the least dignified sticker I could find: four plump bulldogs smoking pipes spelling out the name of the school on the letters of their sweaters. My father loved that sticker.

What I need to believe is that my father did the best he could. He showed his love the way William Carlos Williams described poetry: no ideas but in things. He rewarded my stellar report cards with cash, not praise. He taught me that no draft of an essay was ever good enough. He ferreted out my mistakes and missteps, and his corrections, offered in harsh and dismissive tones, were meant to instill in me a never-resting striving for accomplishment. Maybe it was because he was the son of a violent and angry man. Maybe his rage was ignited by biology and kindled by his own disappointment. I need to believe that my father couldn't help himself, didn't mean to dent and ding me. If he could have been different, kinder, more compassionate, he would have been.

My father craved respect more than he wanted love and risked netting neither. My French teacher demanded nothing. It is his lessons that linger.

RACHEL TOOR is the author of *Admissions Confidential: An Insider's Account of the Elite College Selection Process*, *The Pig and I*, *Personal Record: A Love Affair with Running*, the novel *On the Road to Find Out*, and *Misunderstood: Why the Humble Rat May Be Your Best Pet Ever*. She teaches creative writing at Eastern Washington University in Spokane.

[I Was Mesmerized]

MARIA MAZZIOTTI GILLAN
author

ALFRED WEISS
English, Eastside High School, Paterson, New Jersey

THE PUBLIC SCHOOLS OF PATERSON, New Jersey, were my passport into America. At home I spoke a southern Italian dialect mixed with a few words of English, often mispronounced by my parents in their attempt, unconscious, of course, to make the word more acceptable to their Italian ears. As a consequence, book became *booka*, which for years I thought was the Italian word for book.

At four, when I started kindergarten, I didn't speak English, and I was terrified that I would not know a word or phrase or that an Italian word would escape from my mouth instead of the English one. I tried to be as invisible as possible, spoke only in whispers and then only when asked a direct question. Mostly I prayed a lot that no one would speak to me. But then in first grade the teachers introduced us to the Dick and Jane books, and I fell in love with the story, the characters, and the world they inhabited, so middle-class, so American. If I could have crawled into the lives of the children in those books, with their bright primary colors, their big white house, their wide lawns, their pipe-smoking father, I would have done so. Of course, I couldn't actually do that, but in my imagination I could escape into their world for a little while.

In grammar school, the teachers read poems and stories to us in English, something my parents could not do, and I fell in love with the sound of the English language, the teacher's voices when they read to us. I remember in particular my fifth-grade teacher, Miss Ferraro, who read stories to us and poems by Tennyson and Wordsworth and so many others. Miss Ferraro knew I was entranced by the readings, and I knew she thought I was special, as she was special. She'd walk down the row between desks and she'd touch my shoulder with such exquisite tenderness that for the first time, I was not afraid. I am only sorry I never called or wrote to tell her how grateful I still am to her for making me feel safe and special and for encouraging me to write poems of my own and to go to the library to read as many books as I could.

It was as a freshman at Eastside High School in Paterson that I met the teacher who most influenced my life, Mr. Alfred Weiss. He also loved books and poetry, and when he spoke about literature in his classes, I was mesmerized. He assigned books like George Eliot's *The Mill on the Floss* and Dickens's *David Copperfield* and Steinbeck's *The Grapes of Wrath*. I read every book on the list he assigned, and was hooked for life on language, its power to move us to laughter and tears. For so many of us, Mr. Weiss introduced us to literature in that classroom, where he spoke of books and was on fire with his love for them. How could we not fall in love with them, too?

Mr. Weiss called on me in class frequently, making me, shy and introverted and awkward as I was, feel perceptive and intelligent. Looking back, I think he made many of the students feel that way, but at the time I thought I was the only one. He encouraged me to write and to believe in my writing. He also showed me through his actions that a great teacher is always with us. His voice is in my head, making me believe that a life based on doing what I love is the only life worth living, and I know that my life has been based on that principle, the same one I try to pass on to my students. I think now that he loved us all, and wanted to share his own love of literature with us, and I have tried to do the same.

The story of Mr. Weiss's influence on me does not end there. In about 1980 I had a reading in Greenwich Village. My first book of poems had come out, and I had just started the Poetry Center at Passaic County Community College in Paterson. After my reading, a man approached me and said, "Don't you recognize me?" For a moment I didn't, and then he smiled, and I shouted, "*Mr. Weiss! How wonderful to see you here!*" Later a group went out to dinner, and Mr. Weiss joined us. I learned that he kept in touch with many of his former students, and he filled me in on the students from my class. I was so happy to see him again, and I told him how grateful I was for all his support and encouragement that freshman year.

From that time on, every time I had a reading in New York City, I'd enter the room, and there Mr. Weiss would be, sitting in the front row. He had an apartment in midtown, but even if I read in one of the boroughs, he would be there. He even showed up in Queens during a flood. We had trouble getting there ourselves, but there he was. When I saw him I could feel myself growing taller, more confident. I graduated from high school in 1957. He was my teacher in 1953 and 1954, but he has stayed in my life, arriving at every reading I've given in New York City, with his beautiful smile and his admiration.

Recently, I've spoken to others in my high school class,

and they all have Mr. Weiss stories. He gave them courage, as he gives me courage even today. I recently published a book called *Writing Poetry to Save Your Life: How to Find the Courage to Tell Your Stories*. It is a book about poetry that does not deal with poetic forms but rather with encouraging people to believe that the stories they have to tell are important and need to be told. Mr. Weiss gave me courage, a gift I have tried to pass on to my own students. Brilliant teachers, such as Mr. Weiss, are rare and perfect gems. I am grateful for him.

MARIA MAZZIOTTI GILLAN is winner of the 2014 George Garrett Award for Outstanding Community Service in Literature from AWP, the 2011 Barnes & Noble Writers for Writers Award from Poets & Writers, and the 2008 American Book Award for her book *All That Lies Between Us*. She is the founder and executive director of the Poetry Center at Passaic County Community College, editor of the *Paterson Literary Review*, and director of the creative writing program/professor of English at Binghamton University-SUNY. She has published twenty books, including *The Silence in an Empty House* (2013), *Ancestors' Song* (2013), and *Girls in the Chartreuse Jackets* (2014). Visit her website at www.mariagillan.com.

HILLARY SUSZ

singer and writer

MR. HOLBERT

English, Mt. Spokane High School, Spokane, Washington

BY SENIOR YEAR OF HIGH SCHOOL I needed something else, somewhere else. Kerouac. Beach House. Arcade Fire. A telecaster in the motion of chopping wood. I was taking on the demon of youth alone, establishing solace in self-inflicted captivity.

Mr. Holbert's class wasn't utopia, but it was something else. I remember reading *Hamlet*, analyzing the question of being, *to be or not to be*, and with words simple as grass Mr. Holbert explained a feeling I harbored, that condition. One-by-one he went around the room asking each of us if we ever felt an Ophelia-like inebriation with final loneliness. It was a highly unconventional, maybe inappropriate, class exercise. An outing. When he came to me I bit my gums blue.

I confronted him about it after class. Speaking from my diaphragm I declared, "I'm Ophelia." Clearly I meant something else, hinting at an inner conflict. But he listened and that was enough, and his listening wasn't ordered by the agenda of instruction; it was ordered by empathy.

We became friends. I joined his creative writing club, and he attended my coffee-shop performances. The girl who spent hours holed up in her room practicing and reading was learning confidence: how to put that effort into worldly context.

I can't express what it meant having someone so respectable — an author of two novels, with a degree from the top writing school in the country — not only encouraging but nurturing the development of my work. With Mr. Holbert's guidance I learned how to translate my perspective into something more beautiful. He didn't just influence my work, which he did and still does tremendously (two college recommendations, MFA submission revisions, more revisions, pep talks when I'm insecure, consumed, or stuck); he's the reason the work ever got shared. He saved my life. He assured me that my art has life.

HILLARY SUSZ is a poetically driven songwriter, essayist, and fiction writer living in Boulder, Colorado. She holds a bachelor's degree in creative writing from Western Washington University and is a fiction candidate in the University of Colorado's MFA program. She is a lesbian, a feminist, and, more important, a disciplined writer, listener, reader, and guitarist.

PART FOUR

College

[You're Going to Be a Writer]

JESS WALTER
author

DON WALL
honors English seminar,
Eastern Washington University, Cheney, Washington

YOU'RE GOING TO BE A WRITER.

You have been telling people this since you were eight, when you edited a magazine from your basement and called your collection of comics a library. Now you're eighteen and a freshman, the first in your family to go to college. It is the early 1980s. Your hair is feathered. You've been to discos.

In spite of a lackluster high school grade point average, you land in Eastern Washington University's honors English program. For a while you coast, the way you did in high school, writing essays like "Who's There: Meaning in the First Line of *Hamlet*." Read a page — write an essay — what could be simpler? TV beckons. Road trips are made. A week of classes is missed. You pretend to have mono.

At the end of each quarter you sell your textbooks and use the money to buy cheap beer. The fast-food industry eagerly awaits your graduation.

Then, in the spring of your freshman year, you and your

C-plus average drift into Don Wall's honors English seminar. Dr. Wall is funny and engaging, a challenge to your slacker genius. He assigns a book a week, with an essay due on each. A book a week. You do the math. Ten weeks. Ten books. This is roughly ten more than you have read so far in your college career.

He sees right through your first essay, "Imagery in the First Act of *The Duchess of Malfi*." You get a D. You consider faking mono again.

You meet with Dr. Wall and confess that you are going to be a writer one day.

"You might have to be a reader first," he says.

But you've always been a reader! As a kid you devoured stories: science fiction, adventure. He gives you a half-smile. Clearly he means something else.

So you read.

Dr. Wall helps, infusing discussions of literature with humor and an easy intelligence. He's incredibly quick-witted, with an easygoing reverence for books that you find irresistible. He's an Anglophile, a soccer fan, a mystery buff with a healthy disdain for any sort of canonical snobbery. Alongside Charles Dickens and Virginia Woolf he assigns an early James Michener and Larry McMurtry's wonderful *All My Friends Are Going to Be Strangers*.

He assigns Ken Kesey's *One Flew over the Cuckoo's Nest*, and you are proud to have picked up the Christ imagery of the twelve mental patients following McMurphy to the sea.

But you missed the unreliable narrator, Dr. Wall gently suggests.

So you read it again — on your own! It's amazing, the layers of meaning. You can't stop thinking about it: a whole new world has appeared.

You get an A-minus in his class, and it's the hardest you've ever worked for a grade. When the quarter ends, you keep your books.

Sixteen years later, you are a writer. Your second book is coming out, and your alma mater offers you the chance to recognize a former professor. You remember journalism professors like Bob Alber and Dave Bennett, creative writing instructors like Ursula Hegi and John Keeble, all of whom gave valuable instruction and inspiration.

But your infant son has recently torn the cover off your rat-eared copy of *All My Friends Are Going to Be Strangers*. You hold that book and recall how Dr. Wall woke you up, how he showed you what it takes to be a writer, and the magic that exists beneath the narrative of a book, in the style and thematic subtext. He taught you a second time how to read.

You hold that coverless book and remember his patience, his enthusiasm for language and ideas. You sit at the keyboard and begin to write, the way you have almost every day since wandering into Dr. Wall's class. You're noodling around in different tenses and points of view, trying to find an ending to the piece, when this simple bit of literary brilliance occurs to you: *Thank you so much.*

The essay is published in your old university alumni magazine.

A few days later, Dr. Wall sends you a note: "Many, many thanks for your piece. Frankly, I was floored. Teaching is an act of faith. You do the best you know how, and hope that it makes some difference in someone's life, but you almost never hear back. So your piece was that kind of rare and treasured tribute that every teacher hopes for. Thank *you* so much. You have no idea how deeply that touched me."

Dr. Wall ("Please, call me Don") begins showing up at

your readings. He has recently retired and admits to having followed your writing career over the past fifteen years — your journalism, your nonfiction book, and now your first novel.

"You stare out at those blank faces for all those years, and sometimes you wonder if any of it is getting through," he says. You assure him that it got through.

You and Dr. Wall ("Really, just call me Don") begin meeting for a pint of Guinness now and then. You invite another of Dr. Wall's favorite former students, Jerry White, and the three of you begin sharing poetry and short stories, talk about writing.

More books follow for you, and Dr. Wall ("I mean it — Don!") is always there at your readings. He keeps track of your good reviews and is the first to call when you are nominated for literary prizes.

Sometimes, when you are teaching writing yourself, or guest lecturing at a university, you look out at the blank faces and think of him. ("Teaching is an act of faith.")

When your son begins to play soccer, Dr. Wall ("Are you *ever* going to call me Don?") presents you with a copy of the young adult novel he wrote about a soccer team. It becomes your son's favorite book.

In 2009, twenty-five years after you first wandered into his class, eight years after you reconnected with him, Don is in the hospital, dying of liver disease. You and your son visit him. He is calm and reflective, surrounded by his wonderful family — his wife, kids, grandkids.

As readers, we understand instinctively that every story must come to an end. This is where the meaning comes from.

It's harder to accept with people. We ache for the ones we lose.

Don asks your son about his soccer team. He asks you how the next novel is coming. Hard as always, you say.

"You'll find it," he says. "You always do."

"Rest now, Don," you tell him.

A few days later he is gone.

Teaching is an act of faith.

Life too. You do the best you know how. And you hope that it makes a difference. And when you get that opportunity, you thank the people who made a difference in your life. This is where the meaning comes from.

JESS WALTER is the author of eight books, most recently the number one *New York Times*–bestselling novel *Beautiful Ruins* and the story collection *We Live in Water*. He has been a finalist for the National Book Award and the PEN/USA Literary prize in both fiction and nonfiction, and he won the 2005 Edgar Allan Poe Award. His work has been published in thirty-two languages, and his short fiction has appeared in *Best American Short Stories*, *Harpers*, *McSweeney's*, *Esquire*, and more. Walter lives in Spokane, Washington.

[A Grandson]

BRUCE HOLBERT
teacher and author

ALLAN GURGANUS
University of Iowa's Writers' Workshop, Iowa City, Iowa

IN THE LATE SUMMER OF 1988, at the end of a historic drought, I entered the University of Iowa's Writers' Workshop. A tawny sky fastened to ochre earth, and the cooked yellow lawns and gardens slipped into one another like oils on a palette colored dry. I stepped on a snake walking to the bus. It all seemed a bad omen. My classmates' alma maters included Harvard, Cornell, Boston College, NYU, various liberal arts colleges that had graduated the likes of Paul Newman; some held graduate degrees in law, biology, or film; one was a practicing medical doctor, another the daughter of a famous poet who had grown up on the knee of the department head. My father operated a crane at a hydroelectric dam; my mother was a cocktail waitress. I graduated without distinction from Eastern Washington University, a school that was also without distinction for the most part back then, then had gone on to teach high school English in St. John, Washington, a town of five hundred.

My first month in Iowa, E. L. Doctorow visited. I remember staring at the poster in the department lounge a long while, starstruck. I'd just read *Welcome to Hard Times* and felt a little giddy at the prospect of being in the same room with such a writer. Three of my peers entered behind me, dressed in what was then the requisite black. One nodded toward me. "He probably thinks a bullfighter has come to town," she said. "El Dotorrow." Another replied, a little more loudly, "Don't worry, he will read in English."

They were sophisticated intellectuals who spoke out against cruelty and injustice, and I was a rube they assumed reveled in such inequities. I learned to avoid the lounge and department offices; however, I was compelled to attend class, and this proved opportunity enough for ridicule. Apparently, my peers had determined my brain reptilian and impervious to insult and sharpened their wits on me as boy psychopaths spray gasoline onto frogs then light them and call it science.

This was not true of all, of course. The best writers turned out to be the most decent human beings. Strange, mad, fractured in ways I was and in ways I could not imagine, they bled language and encouraged me to do the same and told me when I bled ugly and when I bled beautifully until I began to recognize the difference between art and confession and craft and inspiration.

My first workshop was led by Allan Gurganus, a curly haired southerner, whose swooping blond mustache seemed part Atticus Finch, part William Faulkner, and part what came before them and part what would follow. The first hour of class, he spoke without rambling, without repetition, with the sincere humility of a perpetual student, the certitude and vehemence of a genius, and the openhearted, irrational hope for his present company that exists only in the greatest teachers. Later, I presented a story that the group agreed had merit. Allan and a few others puffed on the sparks until I recognized what could kindle a blaze and what was already ashes. A few of my tormentors decided their influence had reformed me and ordered shots and beers all around.

At the end of the semester, Allan met with each student in front of a fireplace in his rented house. He served tea and cookies and encouraged me — as he did each of us, I am sure, but separately, to follow our own arcs. He ended our conference with an assignment: write three stories that occur in the same place, but the place is changed in each instance, and the change steers each character in each story. I grew up in the Grand Coulee, a scabland desert split by the Columbia River, both a symbol of nature and of its demise, as by the time I was born it had been rendered a series of reservoirs by several dams; the biggest, the Grand Coulee — larger than Hoover Dam in mass — loomed over my high school, a monstrous presence that provided work for a thousand people.

I put the assignment in a file and, for a year, it didn't enter my mind. Early fall my second year of school, a story of mine was mowed down in class for many of the same reasons my intellect and character had been assailed the year before. I determined to write nothing for the class again in which I had an emotional stake. I happened on Allan's assignment and thought, Why the hell not.

Two sentences into the first story, I knew what would happen two hundred pages later, and I knew all I had to do was keep typing to get there. That manuscript became *The Hour of Lead*, my current novel. It has morphed and cross-pollinated and grown and shrunk for over the twenty-five years since, but Allan's recognition that my obsession with country — it's geographical and cultural force — was married to my interest in people, and how their lives spun out in such places, directed my work from then on. His advice was not a philosophy, which many writers espouse when they teach; Allan stitched his students to their art because he had the remarkable (almost incredible, for an artist) generosity to see fiercely into their work, more fiercely than we could, and, moreover, he saw what we might produce if we could keep the fires kindled. He aimed us toward that end in a manner that allowed us to weather the long, cold winters that temper artists (I didn't publish a book until I was fifty-three, twenty-some years after Iowa) and weed out dilettantes, until the work becomes the purpose of the work, not the impermanent, passing weather of acceptance or rejection, praise or criticism, money or no money, prize or no prize.

He is the grandfather of everything I write, and so many other writers count him as grandfather too that we cannot be numbered. And like a grandfather, he has given us each a portion of himself that is ours alone and supplied us with conviction enough to employ our wares toward our own passions. That's what faith is, really: deciding such a thing is true and believing it; a lot like writing; type a true word and trust another will follow until a story turns inevitable.

BRUCE HOLBERT attended Eastern Washington University and earned his MFA in fiction writing at the University of Iowa Writers' Workshop. His first novel, *Lonesome Animals*, was published by Counterpoint Press in 2012. His second, *The Hour of Lead*, also with Counterpoint, was published in 2014 and was nominated for the 2015 Washington State Book Award. He has taught high school in the Spokane, Washington, area for more than thirty years.

[Made a Lasting Impression]

MYLES KENNEDY
singer

BOB CURNOW
music, Spokane Falls Community College, Spokane, Washington

FAVORITE TEACHER? That is a tough question. Although it's difficult to pinpoint which teacher was my favorite, a few come to mind when I think of who made a lasting impression.

First there was my sixth-grade teacher, Mrs. Johnson, who proved that learning could be fun and essentially taught me healthy habits that I still have as an adult. Then there was my seventh-grade English teacher, Mrs. Robinson. Not only did she help me with my grammar and reading, but she also lent me her copy of *Led Zeppelin IV*, which pretty much changed my entire universe. The list wouldn't be complete without my guitar instructor, Joe Brasch, who unlocked a world of musical secrets that would have taken a lifetime to discover on my own. Joe's quick wit and fret-board mastery kept me entertained and also motivated me to be the best I could be.

If there was one thing I needed to be taught more than

anything, it was to believe in myself. For me, this was the hardest subject to master...by far.

After I finished high school, I enrolled in the Spokane Falls Community College Commercial Music/Jazz Studies program. Though many of my friends were leaving town to go to prestigious music schools all over the country, I chose to stay in my hometown. I knew the SFCC program was great and that I'd have plenty of time to study and evolve as an artist instead of trying to stay afloat in a big city.

A teacher by the name of Bob Curnow had been hired as an instructor by the time I was in my second year of the program. Bob was a big deal on campus because he worked with the Stan Kenton Orchestra as well as having arranged and produced critically acclaimed jazz records on a national level. Having the opportunity to study with someone who had gone into the world and made his mark was something I never took for granted. Though my lessons with Bob revolved around arranging for jazz bands (a skill I haven't put into practice since my days at the Falls), his inspiring and passionate ideas about music and its place in the world resonate with me to this day.

One day Bob asked me into his office to inquire about my future plans. I was soon to receive my degree, so one would assume that I was heading into the world to make a go of things as a musician, but that wasn't the case. I proceeded to tell him that I was considering a different path since I didn't think I had what it took to go farther. After a moment of silence, Bob proceeded to inform me that he believed quite the contrary and that my assessment of the situation was ridiculous. Though it totally took me by surprise, it ended up being one of the most pivotal moments I can remember, helping me to reevaluate my life's direction.

Words of wisdom and affirmation can have a profound effect on a young person. I am forever grateful to Bob and the rest of the teachers who inspired and encouraged me to achieve my goals.

MYLES KENNEDY is an American musician and singer-songwriter best known as the lead vocalist and rhythm guitarist of the rock band Alter Bridge, and as the lead vocalist in Slash's current band, Slash featuring Myles Kennedy and the Conspirators.

I'VE HAD A LOT OF LUCK IN MY LIFE, but certainly among the luckiest was finding myself in Philip Booth's workshop at Syracuse University in 1969. There was this impressive-looking, quite formal man who on the first day of class introduced us to each other, never asking for our input. He had done his homework about our pasts and referred to each of us as, say, Mr. Dunn or Mr. Levis. "Mr. Dunn is a graduate of Hofstra and comes to us from New York City via the corporate world, and lately from a year of living in Spain. Mr. Levis is from Fresno, California, and studied with Philip Levine and Robert Mezey," and so on until all seven of us were sketched. Remember, this was 1969, when formalities were under fire, as were most semblances of authority. In a sense he was introducing us to who he was, and when he spoke about our poems it was a further introduction to his character and principles. Though he was open to a variety of styles, he was not open to anything that smacked of posturing or easy cleverness, or any form of disingenuousness. He had not yet written his wonderful poem "Not to Tell Lies," but he was, in effect, the embodiment of it. One of the most important lessons Philip taught — without overtly teaching it — was that writing poetry was not "creative writing"; it was an extension of one's life, a way of exploring what it felt like to be alive in one's body in a certain place and at a certain time.

I never heard him refer to his mentor, Robert Frost, as anything other than Mr. Frost. I was acutely aware of this, which deterred me from calling him Philip for many years. I think I was in my early forties before I ventured to call him Philip. In those years, between 1969 and, say, 1980, when our relationship was moving toward friendship, I don't know what I called him, not Mr. Booth, but probably "Hello" or "Hi"; those were his names. Nor did he give me permission to call him Philip. My guess is that he rather liked my little dance around the issue of boundaries yet probably was pleased when I could finally call him by his first name. I mention this because he was a man, as you all no doubt know, of very defined boundaries.

For example, in my second year at Syracuse, my then wife and I felt very honored to be invited to his house for drinks before dinner. I remember exactly how he framed the invitation: "Why don't you come around four-thirty and leave at a quarter to six." Philip was wonderful company when he knew the social parameters in advance, and somewhat fidgety company when he didn't. Of course he had the great fortune of having Margaret for a wife. A man could afford a number of eccentricities if he had a Margaret to carry the day. I suspect Philip learned this early, and it became one of the factors in the freedom he felt in being *selves* rather than just a self. Self was firmly rooted; the selves he placed under the scrutiny of the unsparing language of his poems. Margaret, his children, and Castine were the anchors — everything else was adrift. In his poems, especially the ones from midcareer on, he sought to find the words for that elusiveness. They are important poems; they echo the intensity of their making; they testify to a long war between passion and restraint, a war that was constantly being lost and won. He seemed amused by the ambiguities and paradoxes that resulted — that is, when he wasn't being tormented by them.

Over the years, I sent poems to him regularly. He liked some, but when he'd catch me being facile, one of his frequent criticisms would be "Deepen your concerns." You can get cosmetic criticism from many sources, but it's rare to get what Philip had to offer: moral incisiveness, and the conviction that syntax was its evidence. Speaking of which, he hated the inexact, the careless. "That's a shotgun, goddamnit, not a rifle!!" he wrote in the margin of one of my poems. He kept you honest by exemplifying the struggle to be honest. And what's even rarer: the older he got, the more generous spirited he became. For me, a great and important man.

STEPHEN DUNN was a student of Philip Booth in the late sixties and profited greatly from his exacting teaching and eventually his friendship. Dunn has written seventeen books of poetry, including *Different Hours* (2000), awarded the Pulitzer Prize, and *Here and Now* (2011). He lives in Frostburg, Maryland.

[Walter Taught Liberation]

ROSANNE CASH
singer-songwriter

WALTER SULLIVAN
English, Vanderbilt University, Nashville, Tennessee

MY FAVORITE TEACHER was an English professor I had in college, at Vanderbilt University. His name was Walter Sullivan. I took his creative writing class. He was tough and didn't coddle the young writers under his tutelage, but he was also kind and articulate, and extraordinarily encouraging. I don't think I would have had the courage to write prose had I not learned from Walter Sullivan. I am not afraid to take wild turns in a narrative or to allow myself to feel along in the dark for a surprise conclusion, because Walter taught liberation in the same breath that he taught structure. Walter probably has no idea how many writers have been influenced by him. I owe him an enormous debt, and I am tremendously grateful to have studied under him.

ROSANNE CASH is an author and Grammy-winning singer and songwriter. Her fourteen record albums, released over the past thirty years, have charted eleven number one singles. Rosanne has earned numerous accolades for songwriting and performance.

[I Remember the Kindness]

JIM PIDDOCK
actor and producer

MR. CHAMBERS, English, FATHER STEPHEN ORTIGER, history,
ERIC MOTTRAM, American literature,
Worth Abbey, West Sussex, and Kings College, London, England

THREE TEACHERS STAND OUT FOR ME when I look back. And, to be fair to the many others I also benefited greatly from, I probably remember these three the most because they taught subjects I was the most interested in. Or maybe I only became interested in those subjects because of those teachers. Who knows?

The first was Johnny Chambers, who taught English at Worth Abbey, a Benedictine order school I attended between the ages of ten and seventeen. The grade system is different in England, so I don't remember exactly when he was my English teacher, but I'm guessing it was between the ages of about eleven and fourteen. What I remember most about Mr. Chambers, as we knew him then, was that he was more like a friend to us all than a teacher. He was young, energetic, enthusiastic, sporty (he was a coach as well), and, above all, kind. I remember his kindness in particular from an incident when I was about eleven. At the end of a class, he told us our next essay due would be titled "What Is the Value of the Monocle?" Well, I rose to the challenge magnificently and wrote a spectacular essay about the importance and numerous benefits of a single-lens visual aid, with the added personal experience being that I've always had one very good eye myself and one very poor one (after a botched late-1950s operation to correct a squint). When we got the essays back, I was mortified to see that I'd scored an F. The comment attached was, I believe, something along the lines of "Not quite on point, but amusing nevertheless." As I listened to some other boys reading out their essays about the great traditions of the Royal Family in England, it gradually dawned on me that I'd misheard the mandate. The essay title was actually to be "What Is the Value of the *Monarchy*?" I think I had my ears regularly checked, as well as my bad eye, after that. But I was eternally grateful that he didn't make me read my essay aloud or make fun of me.

The next teacher I remember not only for his great enthusiasm for the subject he taught — which was history — but also, again, for the fact that he treated us like equals. This was possibly made easier by the fact that he was a young teacher himself, and we were all sixteen and seventeen years old. His name was Father Stephen Ortiger. He was a Benedictine monk at the school and still is, having since served a term as abbot of the monastery. He also, to this day, remains a good friend and always visits when he comes out to the West Coast for any reason. Stephen *loved* history, and his enthusiasm for making it come alive for us in the present was infectious.

The word *infectious* brings me to the third teacher who made an indelible impression on me. His name was Eric Mottram and, being in love with America and all things American, he taught American literature at King's College, London University. He was also my "tutor," which means that essentially he was assigned to be my guidance counselor if I needed any general academic advice. I remember Eric for three reasons. First, he was a wonderfully eccentric poet with a raucous laugh and an obsession with the importance of sex in literature...which obviously helped any college-age student relate to whatever he was talking about. Second, I remember him saying that teachers don't teach, they "infect." That resonated at the time and still does today. His enthusiasm for literature was something he tried to *infect* students with rather than teach them. Although, to be honest, I didn't really find that out until very late in my university life. I did almost no work at all during my graduate days; I played soccer and acted in plays the whole time.

About three months before my finals in my last year — when you do your entire degree in eight exams — I went through my eight courses with Eric. To his horror, my math was even worse than my industry, and we discovered I'd taken courses for only seven exams. And this is where the third reason I remember him comes into play. Since I hadn't elected to do his American literature course, he gave me a three-month crash course in it. And he was so good that I ended up getting the highest score in American literature in the whole of London University. It made the difference between my getting a very ordinary BA degree (or even possibly failing) and a very good one.

After the results came out, I went to thank him. And, somewhat buoyed by my unexpected success, I asked him whether he thought I should do a master's degree in American literature, under his guidance. He screamed with laughter and said, "God, no! Get the hell out there, Piddock, and do your bloody acting thing. And I expect to see your name in lights soon in the West End!" This turned out to be pretty much the best advice any teacher has given me. Within five years, my name wasn't in lights in the West End, but it was on Broadway...because I'd already emigrated to the country he loved so much and had spoken about with such enthusiasm. And I've never looked back.

I thought about paying Eric Mottram a visit a few years ago, while I was back shooting a film on location in London. Sadly, I found out he'd died a few years earlier. But I knew it wouldn't have been that important to him. The important thing was that I'd been infected. I still read a lot of contemporary American literature. And that would have made him happy.

JIM PIDDOCK is an actor, writer, and producer who lives in Los Angeles. After beginning his career in the theater — appearing in several Broadway shows, including the original production of *Noises Off* — Piddock has since appeared in more than a hundred films and television shows. His latest projects include *Mascots*, an original film for Netflix, which he cowrote with Christopher Guest and costars in, and the dark comedy *Kill Your Friends*, based on the book by John Niven. He's also in the process of creating a new TV drama series called *Faces* and adapting David Lozell Martin's cult novel *The Crying Heart Tattoo* for the screen.

[My Friend and Teacher]

KEN BURNS
director and producer

JEROME LIEBLING
film and photography, Hampshire College, Amherst, Massachusetts

MY FAVORITE TEACHER was a college professor named Jerome Liebling. He was my film and photography instructor, but he instilled in me so much more, giving me a sense of purpose, of mission. Though I graduated more than thirty years ago, he is still a friend, and more important, he is still my teacher, continuing to impart his critical message and vision to a now-aging student.

KEN BURNS is a director and producer of documentary films, including *The Civil War*, *Baseball*, *Jazz*, and *The War*. He has been nominated for two Academy Awards and has won seven Emmys.

[His Dazzling Language]

PETER COYOTE
actor and narrator

SHELDON ZITNER
English, Grinnell College, Grinnell, Iowa

THE TEACHER who left the most indelible impression on me was my English professor at Grinnell College, Sheldon Zitner. A small, round, owlish little man with large horn-rimmed glasses, Zitner spoke slowly and carefully, in something of a high, querulous voice. He made absolutely no attempt to be charismatic, a regular guy, or a good buddy. His tweeds and sweater-vests were a bit musty and fuddy-duddy, and there was nothing hip about him but the force of his mind and his dazzling use of the English language. Nevertheless, he changed my life. It was in his class one day that I realized, listening to him speak, that every word of English was and could be available for everyday discourse; that one did not need to dumb down one's communication but in fact could expand it exponentially by treating the words one reads in books as a currency to be freely spent. I had an epiphany in his classroom one day, feeling the walls of my mind expand almost physically, and from that day forward I have never discriminated between words that are spoken and words that are normally only written down.

His students were in awe of the sharpness and clarity of his mind and often traded "Zitnerisms" like baseball cards after class, collecting and swapping stories about the trenchant observations he would throw away in class like candy wrappers.

Two I remember very vividly. One day, when a student athlete protested the professor's criticism of a certain writer and defended him by asserting that he was "well-rounded," Zitner sighed and responded without hesitation, "Yes, he *is* well-rounded...and half an inch in diameter." On another occasion, during the study of Thucydides's *The History of the Peloponnesian War*, he lowered his glasses, observed the class balefully, and said prophetically (though I did not fully understand it at the time), "Power is always, always, *always*...in the hands of the dumb, the blind, and the creepy." As my life has continued, the value and prophetic nature of Mr. Zitner's comments and example have increased the value of his legacy to me.

PETER COYOTE, an ordained Zen Buddhist priest, has performed as an actor for some of the world's most distinguished filmmakers, including Barry Levinson, Roman Polanski, Pedro Almodóvar, and Steven Spielberg. He is also an Emmy Award–winning narrator of more than 120 documentary films, including Ken Burns's *National Parks*, *Prohibition*, *The West*, *The Dust Bowl*, and the acclaimed *The Roosevelts*, for which he received his second Emmy. Coyote's memoir of the 1960s counterculture, *Sleeping Where I Fall*, received excellent reviews. A chapter from that book, "Carla's Story," won the Pushcart Prize for Excellence in Nonfiction. His latest book is *The Rainman's Third Cure: An Irregular Education* (2015), about mentors and the search for wisdom.

[On a Tangent]

JERRY SPINELLI
author

DR. FRANCIS MASON
English, Gettysburg College, Gettysburg, Pennsylvania

ONE OF MY FAVORITE TEACHERS at Gettysburg College was Dr. Francis Mason. The course was Survey of English Literature. Dr. Mason had a "problem," self-professed: he couldn't stick to the subject of the day. He was always going out on a limb, off on, as he would say, a "tangent." Many times the class would be nearly over when he would glance at the clock in shock and discover that he had yet to cover the poem we had been assigned to study. If he said "I'm sorry" once, he said it a hundred times that year. I wish I had gone up to him after class one day and told him he didn't have to be sorry. His tangents — the fascinating ruminations between the lines of the assigned texts, the stuff we'd never find in a book — kept our interest in a way that no prospectus could. We left his classroom not merely with notebooks full of jottings but with hearts excited and inspired. He did something every student everywhere should be lucky enough to experience: he made us sorry that class was over.

JERRY SPINELLI was born in Norristown, Pennsylvania, and graduated from Gettysburg College. His books are read in many languages and include *Maniac Magee*, winner of the Newbery Medal, and *Wringer*, a Newbery Honor Book. His wife is fellow writer Eileen Spinelli.

[The Man Was Right on the Money]

DOUG HOLDER
poet

DR. SHINAGEL
writing, Harvard University, Cambridge, Massachusetts

At the stroke of eight every lecture evening note-books were spread and until nine o'clock not a glance wandered to the clock nor was there any sign of wavering interest. The students were all voluntary seekers of knowledge who elected philosophy as an aid in constructive thinking. Young and old, black and white, artisans and teachers, men and women — who had questioned the meaning of life, and the universe, were eager to compare their thoughts with the questioners of all time. It was an audience to challenge any professor's attention and respect. (From "The Gates Unbarred," *Boston Evening Transcript*, June 15, 1910)

ALTHOUGH THIS QUOTE is over a hundred years old, it still applies today. I was studying for my master's degree at the Harvard Extension School during the mid-1990s. I was in my late thirties, working more than forty hours a week at McLean

Hospital (a psychiatric facility outside Boston) while attending classes several nights a week. Was it a difficult course of study? Yes. But I loved it. The teachers were first-rate, I fell in love with the winding, tome-filled stacks at the Widener Library, and most important, I gained more confidence as a writer — and I would like to think I graduated as a better, more complete person.

I took a course on the novel with Dr. Shinagel. I remember coming into his office with a convoluted proposal for a paper on Defoe's *Robinson Crusoe*. In his tactful, avuncular manner, he advised me (in so many words) to trash it and start fresh. He told me that it would be a rewarding challenge for me, this nascent scholar. I was doubtful, but in the end the man was right on the money. I was having trouble working full-time and dealing with the demands of academic writing, but Dr. Shinagel (the acting dean of Extension) inspired me to keep on keeping on. I had a number of teachers like this at Harvard, but he sticks in my mind. Sometimes a well-timed supportive nudge can make all the difference in the world.

Doug Holder is the founder of the Ibbetson Street Press. He teaches writing at Bunker Hill Community College in Boston and at Endicott College in Beverly, Massachusetts. His poetry and prose have appeared in *Rattle*, the *Boston Globe Magazine*, *Main Street Rag*, the *Café Review*, and elsewhere. For the past thirty years he has run poetry groups for psychiatric patients at McLean Hospital outside Boston. He holds a master's degree in American and English Literature and Language from Harvard University.

[No More Gold Stars]

KRIS DINNISON
author

DR. DOUG SUGANO
Shakespeare, Whitworth University, Spokane, Washington

TEACHERS WERE ALWAYS IMPORTANT TO ME. I was that kid who wanted the adults in my life to like me. I was that kid who followed the rules and became indignant when other kids didn't. I was that kid who became used to praise and kudos and gold stars. So when my academic career ran headlong into Dr. Doug Sugano, I thought my head was going to explode.

I think my first encounter with Doug was when I took Shakespeare my sophomore year of college. I was not particularly well versed in the Bard, but I'd always had a leg up on the other students in my high school classes. I understood the rhythms of speech and could decipher and decode the puzzle of language into something resembling a story. That had always been enough to garner smiles and accolades and even some small connection with teachers. Our eyes would meet across the classroom as we each acknowledged what the other students were missing.

But Doug was having none of my mediocre fumblings. He knew this material inside and out, loved it passionately. He expected me to dive beneath the surface and stay there as long as it took to find something more than mere stories of kings and murder and mistaken identity. I was to submerge myself and not show my face until I rose gasping to the surface with some tiny gem of true understanding.

I was indignant. And I was terrified. I was sure Doug would be the person to unmask me as the shallow, unimaginative fraud I always believed myself to be. So I dove. Over and over, hiding myself in the search until I learned how to look and where to look, and soon a small pile of lovely learning started to form inside me. This was not the learning of my past, which was concerned with pleasing others and convincing them of my worthiness. This was true understanding, the kind of insight and awareness that might help me really see the world and its beauty and it's big-*T* truth, if I would just keep at it.

Shakespeare was only the beginning. I followed Doug into British literature and writing classes and, God help me, literary criticism, which drove me to despair and nearly undid all his previous good work. He pushed, and I learned, and by the time he was done with me I could no longer content myself with praise or kudos or gold stars. I still felt like a fraud, but next to that there was also this new addiction. I wanted understanding. I craved it. And I could no longer be content with less.

KRIS DINNISON grew up reading books nobody else had read and listening to music nobody else had heard of and thinking she was weird, which she kind of was. She spent nearly two decades as a teacher and librarian while dreaming of becoming a writer. Nowadays she lives, writes, and spins vinyl in Spokane, Washington, with her husband and two cats named Raymond and Moon Pie. Her first novel is entitled *You and Me and Him* (2015).

┌───┐

[Home of the Soul]

SHANN RAY

author

JONATHAN JOHNSON

creative writing, Eastern Washington University, Cheney, Washington

└───┘

LIKE SOME TYPE OF WILDERNESS ANGEL...that's the image I remember when I think of Jonathan Johnson. For six years he taught me poetry and prose. He taught me how to write. He also took me on a journey high in the Beartooth Range in southwest Montana, where he snowshoed sixteen miles in inclement weather, following the path of one of the characters in his novel, just so he could gain a greater feel for the man. In a kind of pain I hadn't foreseen, I only made it six. Then I came down from the mountain to the nearest road and hitchhiked. No cars for miles. High, dark country. The only vehicle that happened by was a forest service truck. I drew myself up into the open truck bed and froze like a block of ice until the ride ended in Red Lodge. I went inside and had a hot meal and thought of Jonathan out there on his own, the stars like silver ingots in the black sky, his large frame trekking happily through the dark.

I'd left him there in that wide-open country over fields of

snow with too many miles yet to go. But he'd simply smiled and said, "Go on. I'll pick you up when I'm done." No bitterness, no hint of shame. He embraced me and said, "See you on the other side."

The other side of what? I thought, as we parted. Walking, it struck me still as his form disappeared into the distance. And when I gripped the metal sides of the truck and slid into the back, again I wondered, the other side of what? Looking back now, I believe it was the other side of friendship he referred to: brotherhood, kindness, grace.

An indomitable bond is formed when the teaching is made as much of life as it is of specific skills one might need to learn. That was him, his own true heart. Happy even under difficult circumstances. He loved life. He loved people. He loved his family. When the older ones in his family died, he helped set them into the afterlife with the uncommon cadence of his voice: gentle and sure, graceful, imbued with fierce compassion, helping people overcome things they formerly found impossible to surmount.

A beautiful poet, an impassioned speaker of the history of poetry, Jonathan was equally adept at the wisdoms of the classroom as he was at the wisdoms of the human heart and the unique gifts that are the result of entering the wilderness. Each of these — the classroom, the human heart, and the wilderness — might be called home of soul.

When he found me in Red Lodge, and we rode together back to our urban lives, his fists looked like red torches in the glow of the dash lights.

His face radiant.

His voice, a voice that remains with me through every wilderness.

SHANN RAY's collection of short stories, *American Masculine*, received the American Book Award, the High Plains Book Award, and the Bakeless Prize. He is also the author of the novel *American Copper*; a work of political theory, *Forgiveness and Power in the Age of Atrocity*; and *Balefire*, a poetry collection. His work has appeared in *McSweeney's*, *Montana Quarterly*, *Narrative*, *Northwest Review*, and *Poetry*. He spent part of his childhood on the Northern Cheyenne Reservation in southeast Montana and has lived in Alaska, Canada, and Germany. A systems psychologist focusing on the psychology of men, he now lives in Spokane, Washington, with his wife and three daughters and teaches leadership and forgiveness studies at Gonzaga University.

ANNIE FINCH

poet and performer

NTOZAKE SHANGE

playwriting, University of Houston, Houston, Texas

I HAVE HAD SO MANY CRUCIAL TEACHERS in my life as a poet that at first I thought it might be hard to choose which one to write about for this book. Would it be my mother, who patiently read my early poems for years — decades, really — with honest, insightful criticism and unswerving faith in my gift? Would it be Dr. Marie Borroff, the first woman to be tenured in the English department at Yale, a peerless role model for me as an undergraduate, with her inspiring dignity and flawless devotion to the language? Would it be Penelope Laurans, who broke open my world by initiating me into the life-changing craft of meter, prosody, and form that I now use daily as a poet, critic, and teacher? Or maybe Adrienne Rich, the great and heroic poet with whom I had the honor of working while earning my PhD at Stanford?

These were all definitely teachers worth writing about. But as I mused on my recollection, the one teacher whose influence sailed inexorably into my mind, the one who meant more to me in my deepest heart than any of these — even than my mother — was the teacher who taught me not only in mind and heart but also in body and soul, during my ill-starred career as a master's student in creative writing at the University of Houston in the 1980s: the legendary playwright, poet, novelist, and performer Ntozake Shange.

I wasn't supposed to be working with Zaki. I had applied and been accepted to Houston's creative writing program, and Zaki was teaching in their theater program. But if it weren't for her, I would never have finished the program. In fact, I might never have started it.

To be taught as deeply as Zaki taught me during those difficult years, you have to be needy. And when I first encountered Ntozake Shange's face on a book jacket, I truly was. I had no idea which way to go, or how to make my life as a poet — or even as a person, since the two felt so inseparable — move forward. The moment in the early 1980s when I first picked up a copy of Zaki's 1976 "choreopoem," *For Colored Girls Who Have Considered Suicide/When the Rainbow Is Enuf* in a Brooklyn Heights bookstore, I had reached a point of desperation. All the supports I had been relying on to suspend me above the abyss — classes and research projects, people and places — had fallen away when I'd graduated from college a few years earlier, and I had no idea that other resources and paths were available. Zaki's book was a seed of wonder and nourishment that shocked me into realizing again how I was meant to grow. Here was a soul-mother, someone else for whom poetry was performative, sacred, curative, indispensable, physical. I held her book close and took it home.

As fate, or luck, or the Goddess would have it, a few months later I discovered it was possible to go to graduate school in creative writing — a strange new idea in 1982. And of the only two schools at the time offering a graduate degree, one, the University of Houston, had just hired Ntozake Shange to teach. That was enough for me. I applied and was accepted, excited at the idea of working with her. Little did I know that Zaki was teaching in the theater department, not in the creative writing department.

Though decades later I would be honored with an Alumni Achievement Award from the University of Houston's creative writing department, as a student there I was a terrible fit. The two core poets on the faculty had no idea what to do with my rhythmic, incantational, mythic feminist poetry that expressed the searchings of my soulful spirit without much representation of the outer world. The first year one of the poets, Stanley Plumly, asked me in exasperation why I didn't just "marry the world" like the other students. The next year the other poet, Cynthia MacDonald, told me that, even after completing all my coursework, I still wasn't ready to graduate because I "hadn't suffered enough yet."

That's when I got an idea. Instead of trying to figure out how to suffer enough to satisfy Cynthia, why not write a thesis of poetic dramas for Zaki? Zaki was delighted to be my thesis adviser; she liked my verse dramas so much that she even quoted one as an epigraph on the title page of her poetry collection *Ridin' the Moon in Texas*. Due to her tutelage, I was able to duck under the sight of the official poetry gatekeepers and leave the University of Houston alive, in every sense.

During the time I worked with Zaki, first as her student in a playwriting class and then as her thesis advisee, her gentle, inspiring influence soaked into my life in a way so unassuming that it was only years later that I realized how profound its impact had been. Zaki, I realize now, was my first working model not only of a successful writer but of a successful artist. Zaki showed me — imperfectly, often, but always with passion and authenticity — how to live in the world as a creative person.

The mother of a toddler (her daughter Savannah was about four at the time), Zaki often seemed to be struggling to keep afloat. She arrived late to class, sometimes disoriented. But I could tell from being with her that she was tapped into her creativity in the same way that I would need to be to succeed in my life's purpose. Zaki was living her dream, following her inner compass, in touch with what I would now call her inner Goddess. After all, this was the woman who had written, in *For Colored Girls*, the oft-quoted lines "I found god in myself / and i loved her / fiercely."

When I think of those years with Zaki now, I still admire her awesomely dramatic hair with its thick, long dreadlocks (a wig, I discovered one day with admiring glee), savor her applesauce-soft voice, and tingle at her charismatic presence. My most vivid memory is of sitting at a book-cluttered dining table eating her homemade chicken soup one evening when I had stopped by to drop off a draft of a play. That night, and many other times, I listened to her talk about the writing life. Zaki lived her writing the way she lived her dancing and performing, out of a core power. It emanates from her words, still tangible, each time I let them carry me away again to places without place.

More than any information, Zaki imparted to me, infused in me, injected into me a sense of the stubborn courage and self-loyalty required to support the long effort of bringing one's unique vision into the world. Now, thanks in part to her, I can say that I do support myself (it's important to say that this is in spite of frequent doubts and fears) the way she once supported me — unswervingly. Amazingly, I didn't have to do anything in particular to earn Zaki's support. I don't remember her offering critiques or information. All that I needed to do to gain the glory of her teaching was to offer her the seed of the true poet she was generous enough to see in me. Zaki told me once, "I believe in you because I can see that you want to fundamentally change American poetry." Lesser poets might have been threatened or annoyed by such an ambition. But Zaki was as insightful as she was courageous.

Interestingly enough, I only remember one classroom moment with Zaki, but I remember it far more vividly than any other moment in a Houston classroom. One late afternoon in playwriting class, Zaki suddenly chose me to play a character in an improv skit in front of everyone: a surly, violent eighteen-year-old boy with a big afro who had just dropped out of high school. I had acted only a few times in my life. But I dove in and completely got into the role, doing a persuasive job, so that the class was truly surprised. It was such an unlikely casting decision for a shy, overeducated white girl that someone actually asked Zaki what had prompted her to choose me, of all people, for the role. "I just saw something in her," she said.

ANNIE FINCH is an internationally celebrated poet, playwright, and performer who has published more than twenty books of poetry and poetics. As a tenured professor of creative writing with a PhD from Stanford, Finch left academic life to found American Witch Community & Marketplace (www.americanwitch.com). Her poetry has been published in *The Penguin Book of Twentieth-Century American Poetry* and performed onstage at Carnegie Hall. Her most recent book of poetry is *Spells: New and Selected Poems*, and she is completing a new book, *American Witch: Five Directions to Your Inner Goddess*.

SHARMA SHIELDS
author

WILLIAM DUNLOP
English, University of Washington, Seattle, Washington

MY JUNIOR YEAR OF COLLEGE, I studied abroad in Spain for a semester. I was supposed to be there for a full year, but I was lovesick for a boy back in Seattle, and, consumed with both self-hatred and relief, I changed my plans and returned early to the University of Washington. My boyfriend seemed grateful enough, but I felt pathetic, knowing I had made a major life decision based on my sentimental feelings for a guy. The effect was deleterious to my selfhood: I grew more dependent on him; I hated how dependent I was. To distract myself, I took extra credits. I managed, somehow, to bully my way into an already full class called Counter Moralities: Shakespeare's *Antony and Cleopatra* and Emily Brontë's *Wuthering Heights*. The professor, William Dunlop, was one of the most beloved in the English department. He was also rumored to be the only tenured professor without a PhD. You understood why within minutes of setting foot in his classroom. I knew I loved him right away when he wrote his name and email address on the board and explained that he chose the username "Eumaeus" because he identified more with the *Odyssey*'s swineherd than with Odysseus himself.

In my memories, which are no doubt flawed, as memories are, William wore the same tweed jacket every day. He was in his fifties, short, and wispy haired, and he spoke in a feisty British accent. His glasses were enormous and he frequently pushed them back onto his forehead as he spoke, only for them to crash back down onto his nose a moment later. When he wasn't teaching, he was penning articles on operas and soccer matches or traveling to Venice with his wonderful wife, Revelle. He brought his outside loves into the classroom and wove them into his lessons, and this is what made his teaching so vibrant. We'd arrive each day unsure of what to expect. He might begin by playing a Rosa Ponselle aria for us — La Gioconda's "El Suicidio," for example, or the moving trio she sang with Martinelli and Pinza in *La Forza del Destino*. Other days it was Schubert, or Caruso, or there would be no music at all; he'd read to us instead, a Stevie Smith poem or a tender sex scene between an elderly couple from a Beckett novel. The range was limitless; we were always surprised, always inspired. He read from a giant hardcover book filled with his own scrawl: quotes from books he loved, poems he adored, the titles of paintings or songs that delighted him. His classroom management was teasingly cantankerous. When a student pontificated, it was not uncommon for him to interrupt, squinting, and say, "Well, all right, Tom, but would you kindly shut up now?" Or he'd cuss-bomb us, always in his warmly acidic tone, "Fecking Edgar Linton and Julius Caesar are tremendous bores, everyone. Bores!" Still, when one of our group disagreed and spoke in favor of Linton or Caesar, and against Heathcliff and Cleopatra (who William revered), he listened to them and applauded them for making up their own minds.

"A good classroom needs dissenters," he would say, "even if Linton and Caesar are fecking assholes."

None of us were immune to his sharpness, just as none of us were spared his generosity. We were on a ship of his making, and we, as his passengers, were simply grateful to be on board.

On Seattle's rare sunny winter days, he took us outside for class. We arranged ourselves in a little semicircle around him, and he chain-smoked beautifully, able to hold a book in one hand, a cigarette in the other, and his glasses on the end of his nose with an unruffled equilibrium. Everything he introduced to us was a new way to enter the texts we were reading, a new way to see the world and make sense of our humanity. As English lit majors, we usually read eight to a dozen titles in a ten-week time frame, and typically we wrote between fifteen and thirty pages' worth of essays, but here we were only reading two works for the entire quarter, and one of them was a relatively short play. William encouraged us to read them each three times. He was teaching us how to read closely; he was teaching us that all our passions are in some way contained within and lifted up by literature; he was teaching us to disagree with the generic readings of canonical texts. I fell in love with Catherine from *Wuthering Heights* and Cleopatra from *Antony and Cleopatra*; William highlighted the following stanza by Shakespeare, and its precision and joy — its gorgeous capture of Cleopatra's esprit and dynamism — make it a perennial favorite of mine:

I saw her once
Hop forty paces through the public street,

And having lost her breath, she spoke and panted,
That she did make defect perfection,
And breathless, power breathe forth.

Once he entered the classroom and barked, "Who said, 'The Sleep of Reason Produces Monsters?'"

Every day held one such trivia question, and I'd yet to answer one. I was impressed with all that my classmates knew, even a bit intimidated. This was an honors class, and we were all honors majors, but I could tell the kids who had gone to public school, like myself, from the ones who had studied in private schools. They seemed more worldly, more aware. The smartest of us was a homeschooled boy, as socially awkward as he was academically robust.

Nonetheless, they were silent here. I knew immediately who the issuer of the quote was, because I'd seen the artist's works many times with my own eyes in the hallways of the Museo del Prado in Madrid. He was, in fact, my favorite artist.

"Goya," I blurted, half afraid that I was wrong, even though I knew I wasn't.

William made eye contact with me as if seeing me for the first time. He asked where I'd learned that, and I admitted that it was sort of a cheat. I'd just returned from Spain, my second visit to the country; I'd seen the very illustration from which the quote was taken. I'd even written it down in my journal.

Something changed that day: William and I became friends. I told him after class how moved I was by the opera arias he played, and he invited me to his home. I brought my boyfriend, the one I loved so bitterly, and we spent a lovely evening with William and Revelle, listening to crackling vinyl and drinking wine and discussing poetry, Italy, music, and our childhoods. William showed us his library, a little room off the dining room, more of a large closet, really, but filled from floorboards to ceiling with books. He gave me an edition of *Tristam Shandy* and encouraged me to read it. I have it still.

My boyfriend and I spent many evenings at their home, and our senior year we went to Venice with them too, for spring break. William took us everywhere on foot, showing us how the maze of streets and canals could suddenly open up onto a plaza or church of breathtaking beauty. They had lived here with their daughter when she was very young. When William and Revelle left some months later for Japan, they invited me to stay in their home for free and care for their cats. The house was beautiful, on a hill in Queen Anne with views of the lake and Puget Sound, but it stank of stale smoke, and as an asthmatic, I had trouble sleeping there. Still, I was proud of the gig and I relished inviting my friends over, playing the operas for them that William had introduced me to, pretending that I was the intellectual I'd always hoped to be one day (and still am not).

Then we graduated, the boyfriend and I, and photos were taken of us together in our red gowns with our honors cords draped around our neck. I was still, two years later, head over heels for him; he had still never told me he loved me. I threw a party with some girls I'd met in a *Ulysses* seminar, and William came and complimented me on my sun hat. I left the evening early, overcome by a migraine. Life continued. I traveled alone to South America. I returned and got a job at the university bookstore. The boyfriend and I broke up. I could always feel his hesitation behind the littlest thing, and eventually I understood that I needed to let the idea of us go.

Two years later, my ex and I met at William and Revelle's house for one last time before I left for Montana's writing program and he left for medical school in Boston. My brother was there too, and some other friends, and the evening started normally, with bottles of wine and records and laughter. I'd given Revelle one or two of my stories to read, and she admired them and then passed them to William, exclaiming to him about my talent.

William read the first page and then said, eyes bloodshot, lips stained purple from the wine, "It's fecking crap."

Normally, knowing William, I would have laughed and promised him something better next time, but that evening I was emotional, distraught, uncertain of myself as a person and as a writer, and I fought back tears. Revelle noticed and reprimanded William, and he looked at me tenderly but said he meant it and knew I could do better. I left the house, choking on my tears, and got into my car and started to drive away. My ex-boyfriend hurried into the yard, waving his arms, and I braked and rolled down my window.

"Are you okay?" he asked. He looked at me with pity.

"I don't want to talk to William again."

I sounded like a child, but I meant it. I was hurt and afraid.

"Stay in touch," he said, and I didn't know if he meant with him or with William and Revelle.

I drove off, crying the entire way home. I felt I was leaving all this behind: my time in Seattle, the pain I'd felt in that relationship, the friends I had here, the cherry trees on campus and the sea-scented air and the rain and the joy of being on my own for the first time. I was in my early twenties, but I still felt like an ignorant young girl, a lifetime away from being an adult.

I left for Montana soon after that; I heard nothing from William and I offered him nothing in return. He was right: my fiction was terrible. It was torn to shreds in its first few workshops. He had tried to warn me. I eventually learned to listen to the dissenters, as he had done in our classroom, and slowly my writing improved. Instead of trashing it in workshop, people began to respond energetically to my work. I softened toward William after a time, realizing how grateful I was to him for everything, how I had learned more from him about reading, writing, arts, culture, and life than any other teacher I'd ever known. I called him the next time I was in Seattle. When I sat with him and Revelle in their home, I noticed that he looked sickly. He wasn't his usual fiery self. He wasn't even smoking. I was grateful to see him. I kissed him on the cheek when I left.

He died two years later. I heard about it from a casual acquaintance, and my knees went weak. I chided myself for falling out of touch with Revelle. I rushed to find out when the funeral would take place, but I'd already missed it. I hated myself that day.

Margaret Drabble wrote an affectionate obituary for him in *The Independent*, concluding, "He was good at endings." She addressed his beloved, if unknown, poetry too: "Why did he not publish more? He was modest and wry, but he knew that his work was good, and he had well-informed admirers. He did not like to press and push."

No, he did not, not regarding his own writing career. But I recall his words to me and their implication: *You can do better.* And I could. And I still can. Press and push.

When my own first volume of fiction was published, by a small press based in Pittsburgh, I wrote to Revelle and told her that I would be in Seattle at the university bookstore, the very store where I worked after I graduated from UW, to give a reading. She came to see me, still beautiful in her sixties, dressed in a simple black dress. Almost no one sat in the audience, but she was there, and my ex-boyfriend was there too, dressed in his medical scrubs (he had returned to Seattle for his residency), and the three of us spoke of William. Revelle gave us each a book of his collected poems, and I gave her a copy of my story collection. My husband, Sam — the true love of my life — was there, and my newborn daughter too. Sam carried her around while I read, and she hardly cried at all. Seeing Revelle and having Sam meet her made my night. And I was so happy that my ex too was there. Seeing Revelle again moved him tremendously. We both had cherished memories of William.

That's the thing about teachers, how kindly their ghosts stay with us. Thank you, William, wherever you are now. I wish I'd told you earlier.

SHARMA SHIELDS is the author of a story collection, *Favorite Monster* (2012), and a novel, *The Sasquatch Hunter's Almanac* (2015). She lives with her husband and children in Spokane, Washington.

JIM BELUSHI

actor

RICHARD HOLGATE

technical director, College of DuPage, Glen Ellyn, Illinois

OUR FIRST MEETING wasn't quite what I expected. The man with the shock of gray hair was swearing and throwing a hammer at the wall. He was building something, and one piece of wood just wouldn't fit. A high school student looking for the summer theater repertory program, I stood in the cafeteria staring at this mad carpenter. He was Richard Holgate, technical director of the College of DuPage, a two-year college in Glen Ellyn, Illinois.

When I graduated from high school a year later, I enrolled at DuPage. By then Mr. Holgate (I have only recently permitted myself to call him Richard) was head of the theater department. He made me his technical assistant. Bent on giving me a well-rounded theater background, he insisted that I stage-manage plays in which I wasn't playing a character. That meant building sets, with him at my side.

I was a bit of a shoplifter in those days. I let it slip to Mr. Holgate that I was stealing tabs of butter in the school cafeteria.

"You know it's not about money for you — it's about getting some kind of thrill. You want a thrill? Run the lights for this show."

He never censored anything he said. In faculty meetings, he'd freely respond to an idea he didn't like with, "Oh, that's a bunch of crap!" In his Film Is Literature class, we fought all the time. He was into Ingmar Bergman. I was into Rod Steiger's character in *On the Waterfront*. He would say, "Jim, you represent mediocrity." I found his honesty refreshing; he didn't want me to change my opinion as much as he wanted to push me to recognize why I held it.

I joined the speech team, and Mr. Holgate helped me come up with a suit for competitions. On weekends, Mr. Holgate did remodeling jobs at the homes of DuPage teachers. Often I helped out. He never took a dime for the work. He'd say, "I know teachers. On their salaries, they can't afford remodeling." When people felt obligated to give him something, he'd say, "Give it to Jimmy." At one house, the owner pulled an old blue suit out of the basement. With the money I got from another, I bought a shirt and tie. My first speech took first place.

Mr. Holgate became a father figure, a mentor, and a friend. I loved my mom and dad, but they had very simple standards for my brother, John, and me — just don't be a bum. Richard Holgate made me work hard and held me accountable by teaching me to be serious about the things that really mattered to me. These turned out to be theater and film.

His agenda was always the same — he wanted to raise our standards in every way. We'd walk down the street, and he'd encourage me to pick up a bottle or scrap of paper and put it in the trash. Even today, when I'm walking my dog, I can't leave a piece of garbage on the sidewalk.

I went from DuPage to Southern Illinois University to

study speech and theater and eventually joined the Second City Touring Company, where I became a professional actor. Mr. Holgate would come to my openings in Chicago, thirty miles from Glen Ellyn — which was really something because he never traveled. I knew he was pleased with my performance if he looked at me and said, "That was fine."

Mr. Holgate is retired now and living in Manitowoc, Wisconsin. Although we no longer see each other much, when we do it's as if we'd last seen each other yesterday.

He will make me sausages and serve them with good beer and we sit in chairs he made himself, and listen to his jazz collection and talk, sometimes for hours. Between visits, if I get a taste for sausages, he goes to his butcher and ships some to me. I try to send him money for them, but he won't hear of it.

The other day I was standing in the kitchen with my son Robert, who is twenty-one. He was complaining, "You're always getting mad at me for not being serious." I said, "I don't care what it is, but it's time for you to get serious about something." Robert thinks I'm tough on him, but I just want to help him to find his passion in life and pursue it. That's what Mr. Holgate did for me.

JIM BELUSHI has been a favorite of film, television, and stage for more than twenty-five years, one of the great leading character actors equally at home in drama and comedy, and a gifted performer who can also hold a room as front man of his rhythm and blues band, the Sacred Hearts. His hit comedy series, *According to Jim*, just wrapped its eighth and final season. His bestselling book, *Real Men Don't Apologize*, was released in 2006. Belushi also commits his time to charities and causes close to his heart, including the John Belushi Scholarship Fund, which services College of DuPage, where he met his inspirational teacher, Richard Holgate.

I Had the Good Fortune to Work with Him

GREGORY SPATZ

author

THOMAS WILLIAMS

English, University of New Hampshire, Durham, New Hampshire

No ONE TEACHER or set of teaching attributes is good or bad for everyone. The undergraduate professor who set Frank Conroy on a fiery path to becoming one of the most celebrated writers and teachers of writing in recent decades, and whose lessons Frank would go over in depth at the start of every semester of workshop class at Iowa, was not the same man or teacher, by any objective measure, by the time I encountered him in an undergrad classroom at the same school, some twenty to thirty years after Frank's time with him. None of that teacher's rigor or brilliance was in evidence anymore. Who actually taught Frank? I have no idea. It certainly wasn't the teacher by the same name who stood up in front of the classroom when I was in his class.

All I've managed to conclude, after these many years as both a student and a teacher is that there are no magic wands, magic bullets, infallible rules, or teachers who can do well for all their students. There are certainly some notoriously *bad* teachers and bad teaching practices, but these are so obvious they're barely worth noting. And for the most part, improving and finally hitting that magical breakthrough in your writing is up to the *student*. Teachers are facilitators or midwives. If we're lucky, as teachers, we're present at the right time with the right sage words and the right tone for delivering those sage words so that the proverbial lightbulb can come on over the student's head.

In my case, this happened just once, my first time in graduate school, 1988–1990, working with the writer Thomas Williams, the last year he was alive. I'd chosen the University of New Hampshire specifically to work with Tom and only learned on my arrival that he'd been diagnosed with lung cancer and was on medical leave. It wasn't until the last semester of my second year, when he had a partial remission and consented to take on a few students as thesis advisees, that I had the good fortune to work with him.

I would say that I met with him half a dozen times over the course of that semester — maybe more.

What I remember of those meetings is that Tom was calm, courteous, and no-nonsense. The first piece I shared with him — my "opus" up to that point in my writing life, a hundred-odd-page novella — he lauded coolly. "It's all there, this thing," he said. "You're basically done with it. Which is very good. It's of a piece. You can stick it at the back of your story collection someday and people will say, what's this big long one here at the back? That's about all you do with it." Then he pointed out a passage he'd underlined in pencil, something about my main character's failure to register his motorcycle or to get a driver's license. Tom rode a motorcycle, somewhat famously, and had written about it beautifully many times. It was one of his signature things. So having his attention on this one detail was just a little excruciating. Of course I'd gotten it wrong. "I mean, why wouldn't he just register this scooter, or whatever it is, instead of always riding on back roads? Make yourself a list of these sorts of questions — it's something I do all the time — and then see if the answers don't help you to find your way."

And just like that, with this one reasonable, practical question, this one bit of scrutiny, I saw my efforts for what they were. A nice try. But I didn't despair, because Tom's advice, to my ears, anyway, didn't sound like cause for despair. His investment in this world I'd created gave me permission to make another run at it.

What I resolved, with Tom's tepid support, was to start again: a new story, beginning with the one thing from my past that I'd never shared with anyone or written about, which was my mother's suicide attempt. In addition to Tom's influence, I had the guidance of writers I'd recently discovered, whose styles and esthetics resonated with me and left me feeling that there *had* to be a way to write something good in my own voice. So aside from Tom, I had David Huddle, Jane Smiley, and Ethan Canin showing me the way. This is important, I think, because whatever a good teacher may do for you, it is ultimately the private conversations you have with the books that move and inspire you that will shape your work and show you the way.

But before all this, before Tom's remission, before meeting him or working with him, there is a day I want to remember, because it also played some part in the breakthrough I was then in the throes of (albeit without knowing). This would have been weeks after enrolling in my first classes at UNH, fall 1988. What I remember is standing in the library at a glass display case of Tom's National Book Award–winning novel

The Hair of Harold Roux (recently reissued by Bloomsbury). In the display case were draft pages, first written out longhand on yellow sheets of legal paper in Tom's neat cursive, and progressing from there to typescript pages, to galleys, to the same final pages in the finished book itself, along the way showing sheets of editing queries from Tom's editor and other correspondence. What struck me was this: the longhand words on the sheets of yellow paper *were exactly the same* as the words — those same words I'd already read over and over, and with so much admiration, months earlier — in the final printed copy of the book. Nothing changed. Tom had had the conviction and clarity and braveness to put those words in exactly the order he'd intended, straight from his brain to the handwritten page, and to hold to that order and selection of words from inception to completion. It was astonishing and daunting and made me wonder not just a little what I was doing there, why I thought I should be a writer and why I had the nerve to ask him to read some of my pages. Particularly impressive to me was seeing his response to the list of line-by-line queries from his editor: "No, no, no, no, maybe, no, no..." Each *no* written in caps, a few underlined, all in black ink.

I remember gripping the edge of that glass case, and knowing something crucial: you must have conviction, and faith in your convictions, and you must be clear. This was all the difference between Tom's work and everything I'd written up to that point in my life: he knew what he meant, and he meant what he said. And though I am still nowhere near as stubborn (or good) as Tom, and nothing I've ever written has gone from draft to print unchanged, I still think back to that display case as a kind of touchstone or dividing line — a beginning point for my own dawning sense of how to be more concrete and definitive.

As I said at the start of this piece, different teachers and different lessons work differently on us all. For me, what it involved was ripping aside all vanity, tuning in to my story, tuning the language to what the story needed, and staying true enough to the characters to find the best possible story shape for them. And what it took to get to that kind of attentiveness for the first time was writing for a teacher whose work I loved, whose vision was clear, uncompromising, and never unkind, and who happened to be dying. That pressure made me forget myself and zero in on what was happening on the page in such a way that I could finally be certain that I was saying exactly what I needed to say; until I could feel the edge of that glass display case under my hand again and hear Tom's voice in my head saying, No, No, No, No, in reply to every imagined question, criticism or doubt.

After four or five weeks, when I'd written myself out on that story, I gave what I had to Tom — about thirty pages at the time. And while I felt good about it, I also felt pretty sure that in some way I'd done my usual bullshit at the end to bluff and dodge my way to a closing line, and that consequently I had no idea what the story was about...also, that I vaguely hoped he wouldn't notice.

But he did.

When we met to go over the pages I saw that they were, as usual, mostly unmarked. He'd underlined a few sentences I also liked a lot, and had written in the margin there, *I love these characters and I believe in them.* He'd circled a few typos and misspellings...and that was it.

"But," he said, standing up from his desk chair, "you are in *no way* done here." He gave me a funny look like he thought I must know this already. "That's the ending? I don't think so. Keep going. It's good."

In my memory what came next is that I literally ran back up the stairs to my office, closed the door, and didn't stop writing until I had the closing twenty pages of the story done. I had all the direction I needed to discover the rest of the story. And by the time I reached the actual ending at around page 52, there was no doubt in my mind: it was done and it had gone exactly where it needed to go, and I knew what it was about.

The last time I saw Tom was in the home of the UNH president, at a reception honoring Tom's colleague Charles Simic, who'd just won the Pulitzer Prize. Classes were done, and I had no money, so I was making the most of the free cheese cubes, celery, crackers, and wine. Tom was healthier, I thought (this turned out not to be the case), if looking a little overheated in a tweed jacket and jeans. I knew from our final meetings that he'd liked that story — "My Mother, Jolene, and Me" — and I felt relatively confident that I might eventually publish it (which I did, about a year later in the *New England Review*, my first publication, and again a few years after that as the opening chapter of my first novel, *No One but Us*), so I wasn't really upset about the fact that I hadn't won any of the awards or prizes given out at the annual end-of-year grad student reading for creative writers a week or two prior. I'd been a little puzzled, because I knew Tom had liked that story, but it didn't weigh on my mind. I figured there was a reason, and anyway, I'd written something I was happy with, something Tom was happy with, and this was a greater reward than any formal departmental acknowledgment.

All the same, our first few moments alone at the snack table, I could see that he was anxious to address this unspoken thing. He kept a hand on my elbow and leaned close so I'd be sure to really hear him. "I want you to know," he said, "that I had nothing at all to do with those graduating awards and prizes this year. I couldn't, because I was gone. I hope you know that."

I nodded. Ate some cheese. Sipped my bad wine. Said something like, "It's okay," or "These things happen," or "I'm on my way to California..."

"But you should know, it wasn't my choice. I loved that story. I just want you to know that."

Again I said whatever I could think of to be deferential and keep my composure.

"Well, good. And you know, the other thing...the thing I wanted to tell you, is that there's really no reason you should stop with those characters. I mean, the story is just fine as it is, but you don't have to stop. You could just keep right on going."

Another light came on in my head.

"You mean—?"

"I don't know what would come next. Maybe it's a novel. I don't know. But you should think about it. Why not?"

In the months that followed, I moved back to California, returned to teaching violin to pay the rent, and went haltingly forward with that novel. Fifty pages in the garbage. Fifty pages lost on my hard drive and miraculously recovered. I also started a correspondence with Tom's daughter, Ann Williams, who'd been part of the same graduating class, though she and I had never been especially close friends. Initially, the correspondence was my way of keeping up on Tom and knowing how he was, but before long — and long after his health took a turn for the worse and he'd passed away — Ann and I were trading stories in the mail, writing lengthy critiques for each other in the spirit of Tom's gracious, no-nonsense, and insightful reading; and later still, propping up or applauding each other through rejections, breakups, divorce, publications, jobs, fellowships, and on and on. And to this day, she is my first and most faithful reader, the one I know I can hit with draft after draft of the same pages and vice versa, and who will always get back to me with useful commentary. So in some way, every word I write, every new line or chapter or story, owes a debt to or has its foothold somewhere back there in that semester of one-on-one work with the one really great teacher who gave me a solid push and whose attention to my work, in combination with whatever other forces were at play, finally made the lightbulb come on over my head for long enough that I could write a good story...and from the brief illumination of that one story, another story and another, and maybe, God willing, a few more.

GREGORY SPATZ's most recent book publications are the novel *Inukshuk* (2012) and the story collection *Half as Happy* (2013). His stories have appeared in the *New England Review*, *Glimmer Train Stories*, *Epoch*, the *Kenyon Review*, *Santa Monica Review*, the *New Yorker*, and elsewhere. A recipient of the 2012 NEA Literature Fellowship, he teaches in the MFA program for creative writing at Eastern Washington University.

[Permission Acknowledgments]

THE FOLLOWING SOURCES have graciously granted permission to use their previously published material.

Page 14, "She Loved the Boys and Girls of Haldeman": Chris Offutt, *No Heroes: A Memoir of Coming Home* (Simon and Schuster, 2002).

Page 65, "He Could Understand": Katherine Marsh, "In Other Words: On a Writer's Journey, Finding a Fellow Traveler," *Literacy Daily*, November 15, 2012, www.literacyworldwide.org/blog/literacy-daily/2012/11/15 /in-other-words-on-a-writer's-journey-finding-a-fellow-traveler-. Reprinted with permission. Learn more about the International Literacy Association at www.literacyworldwide.org.

Page 103, "Full of Thinking and Caring": George Saunders, "The Secret Mansion," *New York Times*, September 14, 2011.

Page 151, "My Journey with Books": Lyrics from Billy Corgan, "Porcelina of the Vast Oceans," from the album *Mellon Collie and the Infinite Sadness* by the Smashing Pumpkins, Cinderella Music (BMI), 1995.

Page 159, "Ignited a Fire in Me": John Glenn, with Nick Taylor, *John Glenn: A Memoir* (Bantam Books, 1999).

Page 163, "And So She Read": Bill Moyers, *Fooling with Words: A Celebration of Poets and Their Craft* (William Morrow, 1999).

Page 217, "You're Going to Be a Writer": An earlier version appeared in the Eastern Washington University *Perspective* magazine, 2001.

[Acknowledgments]

A BIG THANKS TO Georgia Hughes and her great team at New World Library. Thanks also to a great agent, Janet Rosen.

We would like to acknowledge all the wonderful teachers who made a difference in our lives and the lives of our children. They include Jeff Baerwald, Jim Bannister, Molly Beil, Jana Berg, Millie Brezinski, Katherine Bush, Bob Cameron, Carolyn Craven, Carolyn Crossett, Alana Cummings, Larry Curtis, Denise Dalbey, Maria DiBartolo, Ed Drouin, Patty Dudley, Brian Dunn, Maureen Fanion, Mike Folsom, Craig Fouhy, LaShea Hayes, Jim Herling, Corinna Hunter, Kurt Kimberling, Tria Kostelecky, Brenda Kuharski, Joe Lefler, Levi Mazurek, Tim McBride, Camille Miller, Chuck Moffatt, Sue Morgan, Karl Mote, Dave Noble, Dan Nord, Steve Olson, Morris Owen, Dan Peck, George Pettigrew, Jeff Pietz, Robyn Ross, Beth Shaw, Jeana Simpson, Alecia Sing, Angela Spencer, Linda St. Clair, Mark St. Clair, Matt Sullivan, Rob Tapper, Gene Villa, Foster Walsh, Kathy Weiss, Joyce Winters, and Lori Yonago; and the list could go on and on and on.

[Index of Contributors]

Agodon, Kelli Russell, 42

Alger, Derek, 79

Anderson, Gillian, 136

Angelou, Maya, 7

Baker, Joan, 36

Bellos, David, 115

Belushi, Jim, 262

Black, Alethea, 166

Bozza, Anthony, 188

Bridges, Beau, 147

Brown, Helen Gurley, 158

Burns, Ken, 237

Camus, Albert, 3

Cash, Rosanne, 232

Cesarine, Indira, 181

Coyote, Peter, 238

Crosby, Brian, 197

Dershowitz, Alan, 93

Dinnison, Kris, 244

Dunn, Stephen, 229

Epstein, Leslie, 75

Evans, Janet, 31

Federman, Wayne, 155

Finch, Annie, 249

Firestone, Roy, 149

Gaskins, Rudy, 39

Gerritsen, Tess, 119

Gillan, Maria Mazziotti, 208

Glenn, John, 159

Greenwood, Lee, 171

Gross, Andrew, 9

Gurley Brown, Helen, 158

Haislip, Alison, 121

Hardin, Melora, 20

Harper, Suzanne, 51

Holbert, Bruce, 222

Holder, Doug, 242

Hornbacher, Marya, 112

Jackson, Keith, 177

James, Tommy, 132

Kane, Thomas, 90

Karnazes, Dean, 169

Kellerman, Faye, 138

Kennedy, Myles, 226

Klaveno, Mariana, 99

Kraus, Nicola, 194

Krieger, Ellie, 192

Lansing, Sherry, 161

Lashner, William, 184

Lewis, Stewart, 124

Liebetrau, Eric, 151

Lincoln, Abraham, 1

Lyons, CJ, 88

Maguire, Gregory, 33

Marsh, Katherine, 65

Martinez, Daisy, 25

Mazziotti Gillan, Maria, 208

McCracken, Elizabeth, 70

Millman, Dan, 144

Moyers, Bill, 163

Murphey, Cecil, 22

Muske-Dukes, Carol, 44

Offutt, Chris, 14

Perry, Anne, 73

Peters, Julie, 29

Piddock, Jim, 233

Pinsky, Robert, 179

Ray, Shann, 246

Reich, Robert, 68

Rosengren, John, 130

Russell Agodon, Kelli, 42

Saunders, George, 103

Selgin, Peter, 55

Shepherd, Sherri, 27

Shields, Sharma, 254

Shoumatoff, Alex, 95

Simmons, Gene, 12

Spatz, Gregory, 266

Spencer, Stuart, 133

Spinelli, Jerry, 240

Susz, Hillary, 212

Toor, Rachel, 204

Walter, Jess, 217

Webster, Dan, 109

Whalen, John, 140

Wilkins, Joe, 200

Williams, C. K., 47

Wimberley, Darryl, 173

Wolitzer, Meg, 60

[About the Editors]

BRUCE HOLBERT earned an MFA in creative writing from the University of Iowa Writers' Workshop, where he held a Teaching Writing Fellowship. His work has appeared in the *Antioch Review*, the *Iowa Review*, *Other Voices*, *Crab Creek Review*, the *Inlander*, *Hotel Amerika*, the *Spokesman-Review*, the *Tampa Tribune*, the *West Wind Review*, and the *New York Times*. His first novel, *Lonesome Animals*, was published in 2012 and was a finalist for the Spur Award. His second novel, *The Hour of Lead*, was a Kirkus Best Book for 2014 and won the 2015 Washington State Book Award for fiction. Bruce has worked for thirty years as a high school teacher in Jerome, Idaho; in St. John, Washington; and at Mt. Spokane and Rogers High Schools in Spokane, Washington. He has been married for thirty years and has three children. BruceHolbertBooks.com

HOLLY HOLBERT was born and raised in Spokane, Washington, the youngest of five children. She graduated from

Eastern Washington University with a degree in geography and elementary education. She and Bruce met at EWU and were married in 1985. They live on six acres overlooking Long Lake on the Spokane River and have three children: Natalie, twenty-four; Luke, twenty-three; and Jackson, twenty-one.

If you would like to post a story about a favorite teacher, visit the *Thank You, Teacher* Facebook page.

NEW WORLD LIBRARY is dedicated to publishing books and other media that inspire and challenge us to improve the quality of our lives and the world.

We are a socially and environmentally aware company. We recognize that we have an ethical responsibility to our customers, our staff members, and our planet.

We serve our customers by creating the finest publications possible on personal growth, creativity, spirituality, wellness, and other areas of emerging importance. We serve New World Library employees with generous benefits, significant profit sharing, and constant encouragement to pursue their most expansive dreams.

As a member of the Green Press Initiative, we print an increasing number of books with soy-based ink on 100 percent postconsumer-waste recycled paper. Also, we power our offices with solar energy and contribute to non-profit organizations working to make the world a better place for us all.

Our products are available in bookstores everywhere.

www.newworldlibrary.com

At NewWorldLibrary.com you can download our catalog,
subscribe to our e-newsletter, read our blog,
and link to authors' websites, videos, and podcasts.

Find us on Facebook, follow us on Twitter, and watch us on YouTube.

Send your questions and comments our way!
You make it possible for us to do what we love to do.

Phone: 415-884-2100 or 800-972-6657
Catalog requests: Ext. 10 | Orders: Ext. 10 | Fax: 415-884-2199
escort@newworldlibrary.com

NEW WORLD LIBRARY
publishing books that change lives   14 Pamaron Way, Novato, CA 94949